THE 5 DAY NOVEL

SCOTT KING

The 5 Day Novel
Published by Majestic Arts

Cover Design by Scott King
Edited by Leslie Watts

Manufactured in the United States of America

ISBN: 1539136531
ISBN-13: 978-1539136538

First Edition: November 2016

Books by Scott King

Holiday Wars
Holiday Wars Volume 1: The Holiday Spirit
Holiday Wars Volume 2: Winter's Wrath
Holiday Wars Volume 3: Queen's Gambit

Zimmah Chronicles
Cupcakes vs. Brownies
Mermaids vs. Unicorns
Genie vs. Djinn

Finish the Script!
DAD! A Documentary Graphic Novel
National Cthulhu Eats Spaghetti Day
The Eye of Hastur
Ameriguns

TABLE OF CONTENTS

This book is dedicated to those that fear they don't have it in them. Trust me, you do. Go for it!

INTRODUCTION

So here we meet again… unless you've never read any of my books. In that case, what up? I'm Scott King. It's great to have you aboard. I'm really excited about *The 5 Day Novel*, but we need to put our cards on the table before you jump into it.

This book is not a how-to book on craft. *The 5 Day Novel* is about workflow, time management, and planning. I touch upon some craft topics here and there, but if you are looking for something deeper about the craft of writing, then checkout my book *Finish the Script!* or keep an eye out for my future releases. I have several craft-related books on the way!

The 5 Day Novel is structured so that you as the reader can follow the assignments listed within it and write your own novel in five days. I suggest that you first read this book in its entirety, and then, when you are ready to do your own 5 Day Novel, use the checklist at the end of each chapter to guide you on your journey.

I will warn you here and in a few other places: Writing a novel in five days is crazy. There are few good reasons to do it. If you are a sane person, you might gain more from reading this book, seeing how I streamlined my process, and where applicable apply those techniques to your own workflow. With so few good reasons, why did I write a novel in five days? Well, the stupid answer is pretty obvious. I wanted to see if I could.

Over the past year, I've been trying to be a bit more social in indie writing circles. Along the way, I've learned that romance is the hottest genre to write. Romance readers devour novels, and authors, to stay relevant and successful, often crank out multiple books a month.

I've heard tales of romance authors who type so much that they have blisters on their fingers or that they have to ice their wrists while typing because of repetitive stress injuries! I attended an author meet-up once, and a woman mentioned how hard it was to remove blood stains from a keyboard.

Earlier this summer, I wrapped a 110k word epic fantasy novel that took me six months to write. I was feeling pretty good about myself. Then I learned that there were these kick butt romance authors who can put out that many words each month. It made me feel lazy and uncommitted to my writing.

I'm not into machismo and that kind of fronting, but I like to know my limits, both physically and as a creator. Hearing that some of these authors can finish a draft for a 50k-word novel in a day or two blew my mind, and naturally my thoughts progressed to asking myself, *could I write 50k words in a single day?*

I knew writing a novel under such a tight deadline wouldn't be solely about typing fast. It would take extreme planning, quick decision making, and perfecting my workflow.

The more I thought about it, the more I knew I had to try. I had to see if I could write 50k in a single day, but I wanted more than that. I wanted to write a book from concept to polish, and when I estimated the time, I decided I could do it in five days.

The rules for a 5 Day Novel were simple. I had 120 consecutive hours to write a book. There needed to be multiple drafts, and I wasn't allowed to start working on the creative aspects of the book until that clock started ticking. So that meant no plotting, character creation, or any story-related brainstorming until I officially began the challenge.

Even though I wasn't allowed to work on the creative aspects of the challenge until it started, I still had plenty to do that was important for getting into the right mindset. That's what DAY ZERO is about. If you are new to writing, or still trying to find your voice, then make sure you take a peek at it. If you are a seasoned author who has been around the block, I suggest skipping ahead to DAY ONE.

No matter if you are crazy like me and decide to take the five-day challenge, or if you are more sensible and plan to do it at your own pace, good luck. Writing is never easy, and whether you succeed or fail, know that you are never alone.

Day Zero: The Write Mental State

WHAT WORKS FOR YOU

This book is full of advice. Some is based on my personal experience, but most of it is from working with students and seeing what works with them. What you need to remember, more than anything else, is that all writers are different.

What works for one person creatively might not work for someone else. I can't count the number of people who have told me over the years that, if I logged my daily word count, it would help me write faster. It doesn't. I loathe numbers, and when I tried to log my word count, it annoyed the heck out of me and made me write more slowly. Does that mean logging word counts is bad? No, It means that it's not for me.

A large part of becoming a writer is about figuring out what works best for you. You will see a lot of books and classes mention the rules of writing, and if you have only one take away from reading this book, I hope you learn that there are no rules. There are no rights or wrongs with writing. The only thing that matters is finishing your novel.

If to finish your novel you have to write by hand on a yellow legal pad while sitting in a park? That's fine. If you have to get up and write every day at exactly 4:58 a.m. That's fine too. If you like to journal before jumping into your daily writing, there is nothing wrong with that as long as it works for you.

No matter what I tell you in this book, and no matter what anyone else tells you, please remember that the only right way to write is the way that allows you to complete your book.

BECOME A WRITER

To be a writer, you have to decide that you are *a writer*. This revelation comes to authors at various stages in their journeys.

I knew a long time ago that I wanted to tell stories, but because I'm severely dyslexic, I thought I'd make a career working as a screenwriter instead of being an author.

While I was in high school and college, I worked on a dozen or so movies, and for grad school, I was ready to move to Los Angeles. The plan was to go be a minion and work my way up the ladder from an assistant to a working screenwriter. Then my dad, who had been chronically sick, got worse, and I decided to stay closer to home to help out.

It was a hard time emotionally. I knew if I left to follow my dreams that I would regret going. I would always feel guilty that I should have been a better son and done more for him. In the end, I made the right choice for me, but it hit me hard because without being in California and pursuing screenwriting, I lost a bit of my identity.

For almost ten years, it was the plan, and without it, I didn't know who I was creatively. It took me a long time to realize that writing is writing. Even if I couldn't be a screenwriter, I could still tell stories if I changed mediums. That's when I started to pursue comics and novels and started to think of myself as a writer instead of someone trying to be a screenwriter.

If you want to be a writer, you have to decide for yourself what that means. To me, it means that I sit in front of my laptop or desktop and write novels about fat dragons, or living gummy grizzly bears, and books like this.

Lots of people feel that being traditionally published makes them a writer, but I'd like to point out that being published is external validation. Yes, having a book published may make you an author, but being a writer is different. To be a writer, all you have to do is write.

That's one of the greatest things about being a writer. It doesn't matter if someone's day job is working as a lawyer, being a stay-at-home parent, or an EMT. If they write, they can call themselves a writer. It's the idea that anyone can do it that makes the concept of being a writer so romantic. You don't need to be an author to write a book. You just need to write.

Being published or being a good writer are not

qualifications to determine if someone is a writer. If you want to be a writer, then write, but realize when I say that, you have to actually write. Scribbling ideas in a book for three years is not being a writer. Talking about writing, reading books (like this one) on writing, listening to podcasts about writing, or taking classes about writing doesn't make you a writer. Those things might make you a better writer, but to be a writer, you need to write.

When I was in grad school, I met Brad Meltzer. He was doing a book tour for *The Book of Fate*, and I wrote an email to his publicist saying, "Hey, Brad is pretty cool. How about you set me up with an interview?" I have no idea why, but my request went through the chain of command, and I got to meet him.

Brad did a book signing at Politics and Prose in Washington D.C., and afterward, he hung around so we could talk. We chatted for a good hour and a half while drinking coffee. He even invited me to the Free Masons Headquarters for his book launch party. Meeting him was great, and as much as I remember everything we talked about, I bet if you asked him today, he would have no recollection of it.

But that's alright. That's just how these things work, and maybe I would have forgotten the details of our conversation too, except that he mentioned one really cool thing to me. I asked, with so many aspiring authors always seeking advice, how do you figure out what advice to give? He said he always says the same thing. He would tell them, "If you want to be a writer, then write."

I was naïve back then. My focus was shifting from selling spec scripts to entering the comic book scene. At the time, I never imagined I'd be writing novels. So I really didn't understand his advice.

If the conditions were right, I could crank out a screenplay in a single day. I could do the same thing for a comic book script. Neither feel as daunting as writing a book. It makes sense because a script is a blueprint for a finished product, while a book *is* a finished product.

It wasn't until I started writing my own novels that I figured out what Brad meant. Writing a novel is daunting. It's a huge weight that's on your shoulder. It takes days upon days to do it, and when you are in the thick of it, it can feel like you will never come out the other side. When dealing with the weight and responsibility of writing a novel, only you can push yourself into doing it. Only you can make yourself write.

That's the big secret, the magic formula. If you want to be a writer, you have to put your butt in the chair, your hands on the keyboard, and you have to write.

Easy right? Nope. Because as simple as it sounds, people will constantly complain about not having enough time to write. Even now, when I go to events or talk to would-be writers on social media, they constantly say that it's too hard to find the time.

Most people use time as an excuse because it's an easy out. I've used it, not in regard to the act of writing, but about what

I'm writing. For over a year now, I've said that I've wanted to get back into non-fiction but haven't had the time because I've been so busy with my fiction books.

So guess what? I had to make the time. It got to the point that writing another non-fiction book was so important to me that I made it a priority and fit it into my writing schedule. If I hadn't actively decided, "I need to make time for this thing that I want," then *The 5 Day Novel* never would have happened.

I will talk later in more detail about time management, but for now, know that if you never make the time to write, if you never write, if you don't think of yourself as a writer, then you'll never be one.

Assignment: Decide you are a writer.

Why Are You Writing?

There are an infinite number of reasons why a person may want to write a novel. The secret that a lot of people don't know, or aren't willing to acknowledge, is that whatever reason you might have, even if it is different from my reason, it is still valid.

I'm not a fan of writing to market. It's became a huge craze this past year on the indie scene, where writers specifically design a novel to be marketable with the only goal being to make money. Writing to market requires researching what the hot genres are, writing a quick book, and milking it for all it's worth before jumping onto the next hot thing.

But guess what? As much as I'm not a fan of writing to market or teaching others to do it, there is nothing wrong with it. As creators, we all have different things that drive us. Writing to market is a great way to aim for short-term financial benefits. Then if an author keeps it up, building a back catalog, it can lead to long-term finical benefits. It's taking a business approach to indie publishing, and it's a valid way to do things.

I went to college. I went to grad school. I went on to teach at a four-year university. For me, the story and characters matter more than anything else. I don't take a literary approach to my novels, not that there is anything wrong with that either, but I make sure to tell a story that I truly care about. It all comes down to why I write.

I didn't have a bad childhood, but it wasn't picture perfect, and I coped with the challenges by reading books. No matter what was going on in my life, I could turn to Bilbo, and he would be there for me. I could immerse myself in the *Star Wars* Expanded Universe or go on thrilling adventures with Dirk Pitt.

The reason I write is to give back what was given me. I want to create worlds and characters that help people cope and get through whatever might be happening in their real lives. I also write because I can't not write. I go about my days with stories in my head. They are never ending. It's one of the reasons why a lot of authors hate being asked, "Where do you get your ideas?" It's such a strange question because for many creators ideas happen on their own.

If I tried to stop myself from having ideas for books, stories, or characters, I wouldn't be able to do it. It's like when you take a straw and blow into a glass of milk; bubbles froth up and fill your glass. That glass is my head, and on any given day, I have all these stories just trying to get out, and the only way to pop the bubbles is to put those stories down on the page.

These two reasons to write, my desire to give back to readers and writing out of a necessity to clear my head, are great reasons to be a writer, but they aren't any more or less valid than someone who wants to write to market.

I had a student who wanted to write a book about their mother loosing a fight with cancer. They were very self conscious of the premise and didn't like to bring it up in class, especially when I made the students pitch their ideas. I think the only reason they felt comfortable talking to me privately about the topic is because I've always been so open about my father's health.

The student wasn't an English major. She didn't care about publishing or screenwriting. She wanted to write the book because she was worried about her memory slipping. She wanted to remember what her mother was like before her mother got sick. She thought that writing a book about her mother's journey would help not only cement that in her mind, but also be there so that, no matter how many years went by, she could pick it up again and remember who her mother had been.

The student didn't care about publishing, making money, or helping other people, but you know what? She still had a damn good reason to write a novel.

If you want to be a writer, you need to know why you are doing it, and whatever that reason may be, don't let people get you down for it.

Assignment: Decide why you want to write the novel you are about to write.

You Can Be a Writer

I know what my skills are and what I'm good at. I know the things I suck at. Now and then, when I'm not sure about something, like knowing if I can write a good novel in five days, I get adventurous and see if I can. If I fail, I fail. No big deal. It turns out, I'm a weird duck. The idea of failure can be crippling to plenty of people.

Of the hundreds of students I've worked with, there have been dozens who never got started because they were too scared. It happened so frequently that I had to change the way I graded assignments. For the early ones, I placed emphasis on word and page counts rather than the content. Doing so forced those who were dragging their feet to put some words on the page.

The lack of confidence in one's writing ability can stem

from numerous causes. There are too many to try to pinpoint, but the one big thing to realize is that, if you never take the plunge, if you let your fear prevent you from writing, then you'll never be a writer.

I won't lie, it takes thick skin to be an author. You create these things you love and pour your heart and soul into them… and then someone gives you a bad review on Amazon because they totally missed the point of the book. It can be crushing.

I had this happen about two weeks ago. I have a novel called *Cupcakes vs. Brownies*. It is a middle grade adventure story with magic and tons of fun stuff, but there is a darker underlying story about a boy blaming himself for his parent's divorce. The whole theme of the novel is that kids shouldn't blame themselves. Growing up I had a cousin devastated by a divorce 'cause she thought it was her fault. I had friends in the same situation. So when I got my first two star review for the book that said the rating was because it was pro-divorce? It hurt. It's not pro-divorce. It's pro-kid.

Putting the precious things you create on the internet is hard. People can be horrible and undeservedly mean. I've seen writing groups online and offline where the members care more about beating each other down than helping each other out.

I understand why people let fear get in their way, and it is a shame when it happens. As human beings, we all have a unique perspective on the world, and when you don't write because you lack the confidence, that is the world silencing your voice.

The worst case I've seen of this was with a male student I had in a cartooning class. I can't draw worth poop, but I can teach aesthetics and storytelling. So I had the students pitch graphic novels, and over the semester they scripted and drew the first twenty-two pages.

This student was one of the best in the program. He was a fantastic artist. Yet when he talked about his own work, he said it was terrible. He said he would never be good enough. He wanted to drop the class!

I had to do something. His talent was too special to go to waste. Even untrained, his style was developed to the point that he could have been working for Marvel or DC. Yet no matter how I tried to compliment his work or even approach the subject, he would shut down. He flat out, to my face, told me that he thought I was lying when I said he was doing a good job.

This happened in the fall, right around time of the Baltimore Comic-Con. I used to attend the convention to sign books and work at my publisher's booth. I found out my student was going, and I set aside a half hour to meet with him. Together we went around and talked to a bunch of comic creators I knew, and they gave him honest feedback. Most of it was positive, and what wasn't was constructive.

Later that week when we were back at school, I asked him if all those people could have been lying. He told me I could have paid them off. I said that if I had that much money, I wouldn't waste it on making him feel better. He laughed and admitted that not all those people could have been lying and that maybe his art wasn't as terrible as he though it was.

That was five years ago. The last I heard, my student was working in California as a storyboard artist and killing it at the job. If he had let his fear stop him from making art, it would have been horrible. And the truth is, as creators, we cannot grow or improve if we don't create.

If you are like my student and fear is holding you back, the only way to get over it is to write and keep writing. No author is perfect. It is impossible to write a perfect draft. It's alright for your writing to be poop. That's the whole point of rewriting, and sometimes, no matter how hard you try to fix a novel, it can't be fixed. That's how this works. Humans are flawed, and thus, the things we create are too. All you can do as a writer is write the best book you can and try harder on the next one.

In many ways, writing a novel is like asking someone out. Confidence matters, and if you aren't confident in yourself, it shows in your writing. If you don't see yourself as someone who is capable of being an author, then you are setting yourself up for failure.

Assignment: Decide you can write a novel.

NOT GIVING UP

It takes an abundance of skills and qualities to be a writer, but one of the most important is stubbornness. If you want to make it sound nicer, you can say determination, but really I mean stubbornness.

Writing is hard. It takes time. It drains you emotionally and physically. Not everyone can do it. But the biggest thing that separates those who have written from those who have not? Stubbornness.

Those who are published authors make the effort to put their butts in a chair and their fingers on the keyboard. It isn't easy for them. It took a certain amount of stubbornness for them to say they wanted to be a writer so bad that they weren't going to quit till they became one.

I've worked with a lot of students. I've met a lot of indie creators, and it's pretty obvious when you come across someone and know that they have it in them to be a writer. There is a certain sense of hungriness. A sense that no matter what comes along they are going to write the book that they want to write.

Not giving up is hard. We are susceptible to the circumstances in life that keep us from writing. To be a writer, you have to be committed to writing. You need to be stubborn and say that, no matter what is thrown at you, you are going to stick with it.

I knew doing a 5 Day Novel wasn't going to be easy. It would take a lot of work, and even if I made the commitment and put in the crazy hours, I could still fail. I didn't decide to attempt it until the weekend before I jumped in.

My wife, Lisa, gave me a thumbs up for the idea. And beyond that, I made sure I went public with what I was about to do. I put it on my blog, Twitter, and Facebook. I wasn't bragging, saying something like "I'm so awesome, and I'm going to write a book in five days." I was honest and basically said, "I'm going to do this crazy thing. I may crash hard, so why don't we find out together if I can do it?"

For me, accountability was huge. By making it public, I couldn't get through the first day and be like "uh this is too hard, I'm going to quit."

Now that I've been through the trenches and am well on the other side of having written a novel in five days, I can promise you it's brutal. I practically broke my brain multiple times. You know when people get punch-drunk from lack of sleep? I was like that even though I made sure I got rest and exercise every day.

The grueling mental capacity it takes to create a novel in five days and then shape it so it looks no different from a novel written in thirty or more… it's crushing. I was able to do it only out of sheer stubbornness. No matter how quickly you plan to write a novel, if you give up, you'll never finish.

Assignment: Make a commitment to your writing, promising to stick with it until it's done.

MAKING TIME

The 5 Day Novel is intense. It's like crawling into a black hole, being thrown about, having your brain fried, and coming out on the other side blinking, confused, and saying, "Wait, what day is it?"

I said in the introduction of this book, and I'm going to say it again here: After having written a novel in five days, I don't think you should do it. The time commitment alone is savage. When you factor in the mental and physical tax you have to pay to get it done, well, it's not for everyone.

Of the one hundred and twenty consecutive hours, ninety to ninety-five were spent writing. The rest of the time was dedicated to sleeping or doing a daily walk. That means for five days I basically breathed the book. If you can type faster than I can, your mileage may go better. Maybe it would take you only eighty hours or even seventy? Still that is a huge time commitment.

If you can't commit to upwards of one hundred hours over a five-day span, then that's alright. Doing a 5 Day Novel isn't for everyone. But you need to ask what you can commit to. Can you do ten hours a day? Five? Two? Figure it out. Make that time and write. As long as you keep writing, you'll eventually finish. Even if you work only an hour a day, that means that in a hundred days you should have a finished novel!

I know making time isn't easy. I make half my income from books and half from board game photography. It's a weird balance and means about half my day is spent writing. I take a break for lunch, exercise, and spend afternoons shooting games for clients or working on publishing and marketing.

You have only so many hours in a day. If you are trying to find time to write your novel, then the easy answer is to tell you to get up an hour earlier and make that your writing time.

The problem with getting up early is that some people have schedules that are so packed that getting up an hour earlier isn't possible. It might make the difference between six hours of sleep and five. If you can't start your day earlier or end it later, then the only other option is to find the time somewhere in the middle.

I mentioned before that I have been wanting to get back to writing nonfiction. Since moving to Texas three years ago, I gave up teaching college to follow my wife's job, and I miss it. I miss working with students and seeing them grow. It's not the same, but doing nonfiction gives me back a bit of that joy.

In the spring I tried to set it up so that the hour from five to six in the evening would be dedicated to nonfiction. It didn't work. Something always came up. I thought about getting up an hour earlier to do nonfiction, but my schedule is so full that losing that hour of sleep would break me.

It meant that if I wanted to write nonfiction, I would have to fit it in another way. Ultimately, I had to look at all the side projects I was working on, and I ended up having to shelve one I love.

For three years, I've been doing a podcast called The Creators Cast. I get no income from it, but it's something I do more out of love than anything else. On the show I get to talk to authors, voice actors, artists, app developers, photographers, and any cool person who makes stuff.

The problem with the podcast is that editing and uploading the episodes is a time hog. When I had sat down to prioritize my schedule, I realized that although I love doing the show, writing a nonfiction book was more important to me.

If you want to be a writer and are trying to fit writing into an already packed schedule, then chances are you will have to give something up to make time for it. Maybe you skip watching TV at night, or you give up a half hour of reading, or you swear off social media for a month? Time is what it is. You can't add more hours in the day, and if being a writer truly matters to you,

you have to make it a priority.

It's not all doom and gloom. My podcast? It's not dead. I've secretly spent this past summer recording episodes. I've had time to chat with cool people. I've not had the time to edit and post them. So my solution has been to save up a bit of money and hire a virtual assistant to do that for me. Yes, it means I'm losing on money, but it also means I get to have my cake and eat it too. I get to write nonfiction, and come this fall, I'll take the podcast off hiatus.

If you want to be a writer, if it truly matters to you, then you need to make time for it. Whether you do it by adjusting your sleep, recreation, or free time, it all comes down to the fact that, if you don't make the time to write, then you will never have written.

Assignment: No matter if you plan to do it in five days or thirty, make the time to write your novel.

Take Care of Yourself

If, by some miracle, you have a hundred and twenty consecutive hours and are going to attempt a 5 Day Novel, understand it's a bit more than clearing your schedule.

For example, I honestly don't think I could have done it without first getting Lisa's blessing. She had to understand and know that, when she was home and I was writing, I had to write. That's a big difference from how I normally work. She is a chemical engineer and does twelve- to fourteen-hour days. Our normal rule is that, if she is at work, then I'm at home working, but when she's home, I spend time with her.

I do it because, to me, family is a priority. As much as I love photography, writing, and making money, if I don't get to spend time with her, it's not worth it. Plus, going on adventures with her charges me up so that I can work hard when she's not there.

Lisa was skeptical at first about the 5 Day novel. She had heard stories about romance novelists soaking their hands in ice buckets and having to cope with bloody blisters. She thought I was more than capable of writing a book in five days, but she didn't want me to get hurt while doing it.

We had to strike a deal. She demanded that I eat three meals a day and have healthy snacks between those meals. I had to do my daily five-mile walk, and every seventy-five minutes, I had to get up and move around the house. She also required that I sleep every night.

I've been doing the freelance writer and photography thing for years now. I have my system. It's easy for me to sit down for five hours a day and write. If you are new to writing, that won't be easy for you. It's like exercising. An out of shape person can't wake up one morning and say, "Hey, I'm going to run a marathon today," and then do the marathon without any problems.

When I looked into how long it takes a novice runner to get in shape for a marathon, most of the plans I saw created an eighteen- to thirty-week training schedule. Just like a person would need to train and get ready for such a daunting task, if you are a new writer, you need to do the same to get your brain and habits in shape before attempting a 5 Day Novel.

Our bodies are machines. They require things like food, water, and sleep. If you plan to push yourself and do a crazy thing like write a novel in five days, you need to understand that the only way you will succeed is if you take care of yourself while doing so.

KNOW YOUR VOICE

Two types of voice appear in novels. Individual characters have specific voices, and the author has a unique voice too. It's the author's voice that I'm referring to in this chapter.

Voice is one of the hardest things to teach because it's not something you can teach. The author develops this over time, and it is what makes one different from the hundreds of other authors out there.

What makes you, you?

Let's pretend you create a character. We will say she is an eighty-year-old, white woman. She is ex-military and designed submarines for the Navy back in the day. Even now, decades after she's retired, she won't talk about her job because her work is still classified.

As an author, how would you decide what that woman's voice was like? Well, you'd analyze her. We can tell from the brief description that the woman is smart. We know how women were treated back then and can guess she must be tough or at least have a thick skin.

To figure out her voice, you would take everything that is her and try to imagine the world from her point of view. That's kind of what it's like to find your author's voice. What makes my voice different from your voice is all of my life experience and my point of view or the way I see the world.

My voice is tied to humor and is also hopeful. No matter how bad things get for my characters, I always include a bit of joy. That's because it's who I am as a person.

Not only will embracing your voice make you a better author, but it will also help you during the writing process. My education and taste lean toward screenwriting. That means when I write a book I don't like points of view (POV) that are too deep. I also end up underwriting descriptions because the action lines you see in a screenplay are so skimpy compared to the narrative prose you see in a novel.

The effect of tighter descriptions in my novels and the POV I prefer means my books often read fast. It makes me better suited to write a thriller or adventure story as opposed to a slower paced drama.

Because I know my voice, I went into my 5 Day Novel knowing that the descriptions would be on the lighter side. It meant that, if I was aiming for 50k words for the finished novel, then the first draft would probably be around 40k words. As I did rewrites, adding in more description and fleshing out the POV, the word count would creep up.

The only way to know your voice as a writer is to write. As you develop the way you deal with pacing, structuring a scene, and all the stuff that goes into a book, your voice will start to take shape. Once you have several books under your belt, you'll start to recognize who you are as a writer, and when you do that, you should gravitate to the elements of your unique style.

There is no magic button to find your voice. It takes time and practice. It takes growth. But you can start paying attention to it and being aware of it. Other than finishing your novels, finding your voice as an author might be the single hardest thing to do.

I took a writing class with *New York Times* best-selling author Mary Robinette Kowal. There were seven of us in the class, and we all had varying backgrounds and experience. As an exercise, she gave us a scene in which the dialog was all pre-written. She told us that it was two characters speaking and that we couldn't change any of the dialog.

We were given about an hour then had to swap scenes and read them. Mine ended up being a dark fantasy story about catty high school girls trying to summon a wicked elder god. That's very in line with who I am as an author.

One of the other students turned the scene into a story

about a woman in a fantasy world sacrificing her best friend to bring back her dead husband. A third student made it an epic space scene between two miners working on a remote planet.

The reason all those stories came out so different, even though they had the exact same dialog, is that as authors, we all have different voices. Your voice affects sentence structure, word choice, the way you handle scene transitions, and just about everything else.

If you don't already know your voice, there is nothing you can do to find it overnight, but keep an eye out and know that the more you write, the clearer your voice will become.

Assignment: Be aware of what an author's voice is and start trying to figure out what yours might be.

Write What You Know

I hate when people say, "Write what you know." It's stupid. I also think it's totally right, but most people misunderstand its meaning.

I have never visited a candypunk world where countries are at war and trying to kill each other with weaponized desserts. That didn't stop me from writing my book *Cupcakes vs. Brownies*.

You see, writing what you know isn't about writing the things that are literally *of your life*. It's an all-encompassing phrase.

I love middle grade novels. I have always loved them. I was reading Harry Potter when the first book came out, and I did the same with the Percy Jackson series.

Although I personally have never been on a zeppelin airship made from dark chocolate brownies, I know the middle grade genre and, thus, knew I could write a story set in that genre.

Let's look at the reverse of that. I have never read a romance novel. I don't hate the genre, it's just never been my thing. Even though I know writing romance can be very lucrative as an author, it would be stupid for me to do so. I could write a book with romance in it, but not a romance novel. When choosing to write a novel, you need to write in a genre that you understand. If I tried to write a romance, I would fail.

Think back to when we were talking about your voice as an author. Your voice is your unique POV on the world. I grew up with a sick parent. It's easy for me to write about what it is like and the emotional state that situation evoked. Does that mean someone who didn't grow up with a sick parent can't write about that? No, of course not. It's just easier for me 'cause I can draw from my own life experience. So when you're deciding on what kind of story you want your novel to be, think about some of the things that make you unique as a person.

I write at a coffee shop called Brew-n-Bake. In the mornings, one of the regulars, whom I'll nickname Navy-Mark, 'cause he's retired Navy, always comes over and chats. You'd think it would be a distraction, but Navy-Mark has a ridiculous number of stories. Talking to him is refreshing because he shares a point of view on life and draws upon experiences that are drastically different from my own.

I can't count the number of times he's told me a story that included, "I thought we were going to die." Not even talking about a wartime situation or something Navy related. My favorite

Navy-Mark story is one from when he was a teenager in the Boy Scouts.

He and a buddy were walking in the woods, and they came across a javelina, which is like a wild boar but smaller and more aggressive.

The javelina made a snorting sound and charged Navy-Mark and his friend. They were unarmed. The beast had jagged tusks and could easily outrun them. Navy-Mark thought they were goners, but as they fled, they found a tree big enough to hold them. They scrambled up into it, and once safe, they sat there, hoping the demonic critter would leave.

Instead of leaving, the javelina beat its tusks against the tree's trunk as if trying to knock it over. About twenty-five minutes later, it keeled over and went limp. Navy-Mark and his friend weren't sure if it had knocked itself out or if it had beaten itself to death. In a very stupid-teen way, Navy-Mark's friend asked, "Should we poke it with a stick?"

Navy-Mark talked his friend out of poking the deadly creature with a stick, and instead they jumped out of the tree and ran for their lives. The next morning, they returned to the location and saw that the javelina still lay there—dead. It had killed itself trying to get them!

If Navy-Mark came to me and said he wanted to write a novel, I wouldn't tell him that it had to be military related, but knowing him, I would say that it had to have humor and adventure because that's who he is. That's the life he has lived, and it's what he knows.

So what happens if you want to write a book about something that you don't know or have experience with? Then you have to learn.

I knew going into The 5 Day Novel challenge that I wanted to write a book that in some way thematically touched upon gun violence. It's a huge topic that has become ultrasensitive in the past two years. The problem is that I have shot a gun only once in my life. I was nine. My only other experience with guns is what I've seen in video games or movies, which means I know nothing about guns.

If I followed the normal understanding of "write what you know," I'd have to give up writing about guns, but that's stupid, because it was a topic I was very interested in exploring. Instead of dropping the idea, I simply had to educate myself.

I started online, reading about different kinds of guns. I learned the difference between a 9 mm and a 50 cal. I read federal laws. I read state laws. I watched hours of YouTube videos on how to handle a gun properly, how to aim one, how to dismantle one, and how to load one. That wasn't enough though. I still couldn't write about guns with any sense of authority.

At that point, I had to expand my research. The obvious thing would be to go to a range or take a class. I wasn't into doing that, so I decided to talk to real people. I spoke to two police officers, which was hard because it was less than a week after the tragic sniper shooting in Dallas, Texas. I interviewed two ex-military service members. I talked with two gun owners and an anti-gun advocate.

When all was said and done, not only did I feel confident enough to write about characters using guns, but the wide breath of people I talked to meant that I also could write about characters with different opinions and backgrounds.

When an author puts out a book on a topic they don't know, it's clear. Our life makes us who we are, and it's ok not know something, but if you don't know and want to write about a topic, then educate yourself first.

Assignment: Decide what you want to write about, and if you don't know the subject well enough to write with authority, then learn more about it.

DAY ZERO JOURNAL

This is the blog post I wrote the weekend before attempting my 5 Day Novel…

I'm aiming to write a 50k-ish-word novel this week. That's from concept to polish with at least two rewrites built in.

I have no idea if I will be able to do it. I'm a bit nervous. I'd like to do it secretly and not tell anyone so if I fail, then no one will know. However, I think that is cheating. So I'm making it public.

Right now I know that the book will be thriller. It will most likely be an action thriller. I know I want the protagonist to be an FBI agent. Outside of that, I've not done any planning. I'll figure that all out tomorrow once I officially start working.

I have spent the past week researching the FBI, gun types, jurisdiction between feds and police, and those kinds of things. Just to make sure I know enough to write competent characters. I have not done any story or character planning yet.

I'll *try* to put an update here everyday, though they may be short 'cause I'm going to be a bit busy. Plus, I'm going to unplug my router so I can avoid social media and the web in general. They can be a bit of a distraction. But every night, or maybe when I do my daily walks, I'll try to post updates!

DAY ZERO CHECKLIST

- **Assignment:** Decide you are a writer.
- **Assignment:** Decide why you want to write the novel you are about to write.
- **Assignment:** Decide you can write a novel.
- **Assignment:** Make a commitment to your writing, promising to stick with it until it's done.
- **Assignment:** No matter if you plan to do it in five days or thirty, make the time to write your novel.
- **Assignment:** Be aware of what an author's voice is and start trying to figure out what yours might be.
- **Assignment:** Decide what you want to write about, and if you don't know the subject well enough to write with authority, then learn more about it.

Day One: Prewriting

SPOILER ALERT

As you continue to read *The 5 Day Novel*, you will find spoilers for *Ameriguns*, the novel I wrote in five days. If you are not a fan of spoilers, I suggest you pick it up, read it, and come back here to see how I wrote it. If you don't care about spoilers, then keep on trucking...

Day One Plans

DAY ONE is all about prewriting. It's all the work you need to do before you start the actual writing process. This includes coming up with the story's concept, characters, setting, and the plot, in other words, all those creative things are dreamed up during the prewriting stage.

I could have started writing my novel on DAY ONE, but since one of my main goals for doing the 5 Day Novel was to see how many words I could write in a single day, I wanted to wait until the morning of DAY TWO before starting. If you are a crazy person who is trying to do a 5 Day Novel, I suggest you start writing as soon as you finish the prewriting. If you are taking your time and writing more of a fifteen or thirty-day novel, then don't feel pressured to jump right in on DAY ONE.

Forming the Idea

Going into the challenge, I knew I wanted to touch upon gun violence, and so it made sense to make my 5 Day Novel a thriller and to have the protagonist be an FBI agent.

In all the books, screenplays, and comics that I have written, I have never started with a theme. So it was very strange to jump into the challenge knowing my theme but not knowing the characters or premise.

After doing all the research and talking to many people about guns, I wasn't sure which way to take the theme. I knew I wanted to explore it, but that was it. So the first thing I had to decide was what my overall point was. Why was I writing this book?

On the surface, my goal was to see if I could write a good

novel in five days, but because I'm someone who cares about story and characters, that's not enough motivation for me. If I spend time writing something, I need to really care and feel passionate about some aspect of the story.

I've heard a saying in movies and on TV shows before that goes like this: "The definition of an insane person is repeating the same action over and over again and expecting different results." I don't know how accurate that is. I've never actually checked the *DSM-5*, but I like the concept and think it applies to gun violence.

If we do nothing, then nothing will change. I don't know what should be done, but I don't need to know or have the answer. I needed to decide what my theme was, and that was it. The point I wanted to stress in the underlying message of the novel was that nothing will change if we don't change it.

With that in mind, it was pretty easy to come up with a title and high concept idea for the novel. Right away I thought of "Ameriguns" and figured there was no way to tiptoe around the subject. I needed to focus on mass shootings and police violence, but I couldn't just throw social problems into a story like that. To handle such sensitive issues, I would need to put the character and plot first and have the theme flow beneath the surface.

To make the novel writing process as simple as possible, I decided to set the book in Washington, D.C., I spent half my childhood and went to grad school there. I know D.C., and it has a vibe that makes it perfect for a story about politics, laws, and the government.

Not only would the setting fit the story, but because I love D.C., and have spent so much time there, it would be easy to set the story there. I've passed by the townhouses along M Street. I've driven through Embassy Row hundreds of times. I used to walk two blocks from my apartment to go to the National Cathedral.

By setting the novel in Washington, D.C., I wouldn't have to waste any time researching a new location. It was a shortcut for world building but one that also fit the theme.

One of the police officers I interviewed for the book had told me that post 9/11 everyone in law enforcement was worried about terrorist cells. Tons of movies and TV shows depict groups of terrorists working to do something horrible, but now a days, because of monitoring and tracking, it's not the groups of people who are the real threat. It's the single individuals who fly under the radar who can cause the most damage.

The concept really stuck with me, and once I knew the theme and the location of my 5 Day Novel, I decided that Ameriguns, in the book, were lone gunmen who kept committing random mass shootings in the city. Since I knew I wanted to write a thriller, it meant my protagonist would be an FBI agent trying to stop them.

Working from theme to high concept was a backward way of doing things, but it worked. Chances are, if you are like most people, a character, character arc, or high concept will jump out at you first. Whatever that idea is, your first task is to flesh it out.

Take your ideas, swish them around, and when you've finished, decide upon a basic concept for your novel. Make sure you know where you are going to set the story and why it's a story you want to tell.

Assignment: Form the main idea for your novel.

PICKING A GENRE

In screenwriting, structure is key. You can tell whatever story you want to tell, but it must fit into the traditional three act structure to be commercially viable. In novels, however, genre is king.

Picking a genre and adhering to it ties into reader expectation. If you were to write an epic fantasy novel, and the last third of the book contained the conventions of a historical sci-fi romance, it would upset your readers. The epic fantasy lovers would be furious about how it ended, and the historical sci-fi romance fans would never read far enough to get to the stuff they would like. It's not that genre mash-ups can't work, it's that shifts in genre that aren't properly set up feel unsatisfying.

Reader expectation is powerful, and it's all based on what the author does in the early pages of a novel. When a new reader picks up a book, they start to see promises. If your novel begins with a huge action sequence, then you are making a promise to the reader that your book is going to be an action book. If you don't deliver any more action after that first scene, you are sending the wrong message.

Remember our discussion on writing what you know? Romance novels have strict rules for how the genre works. Since I don't read romance, if I tried to write a romance novel, I would most likely break the majority of the rules. I would make promises at the start of the novel, and because I didn't know the what is expected, I would break those promises later, which would lead to a bad experience for the readers.

The main fiction genres listed on Amazon are children's books; literature & fiction; mystery, thriller & suspense; romance; science fiction & fantasy; and teen & young adult. Each of those main genres have subcategories. For example, under fantasy, you'll find alternate history, Arthurian, coming of age, dark, epic, and half a dozen others.

In my case, I knew that I wanted *Ameriguns* to be a thriller. I read a lot of fantasy and middle grade books, but I also read thrillers, so I'm qualified to write one. The question I'm left with, though, is what kind of thriller do I want to write? There are crime thrillers, historical thrillers, legal thrillers, supernatural thrillers, and a bunch of others.

I would like to do a darker crime thriller. Something more Lee Childs-like or James Patterson-ish, but I know me, and although I can do dark, I have trouble with gritty. Most of the thrillers I read are either adventure based or political, so a novel more along the lines of what Brad Meltzer or Steve Berry would write is probably more my style and better fits my voice.

I want to tell a story that has action, gun fights, and political intrigue. As serious as the topic of gun violence is, I don't want to have to get into the headspace to write a novel that is like *Silence of the Lambs* or *Seven*-ish.

Picking your genre can be a daunting task. If you're stuck, stop and think about the story you want to tell. What fits you? What kind of books do you read, and what subgenre might work well with how you naturally tell stories? Try not to worry too much about categories and instead focus on authors in the genre who's tone is one you would like to emulate.

Assignment: Pick the genre(s) your novel will fall into.

PROTAGONIST

Normally when I decide what kind of story to write, I start with character. I hear a voice and get a sense of the journey they will have. It's very different for me to create a character to fit the story I'm telling.

I know from reading thrillers that a lot of the protagonist are white, male, and straight. That seemed boring to me, and it wouldn't offer an interesting point of view on police violence.

Since my goal for the book was more about exploring certain themes, I had to consider what type of character would meet my needs best. Right away, I settled on a gay, black, and male character.

With the high number of police officers shooting unarmed black males, it seemed like a given. If I wanted to explore that aspect of gun violence, I either had to make my protagonist a victim of such a situation or the person who caused the situation.

I settled on a gay character 'cause it interested me. It's not a character you often see in that capacity in novels, and there is no reason why you couldn't have a non-heterosexual character in that role. I can't remove prejudice from the real world, but if I can have more diversity in my novels, I'm all for that.

Lead characters in thrillers always seem to to have a tough sounding name. Something like Jack Stonebrick, which oozes manliness. I settled on Nathaniel Ryder for my protagonist. As an FBI agent, it meant anyone at work would be calling him Ryder or "Agent Ryder" and I liked Nathaniel. It has an almost geekyness to it.

Once I could picture Nathaniel Ryder in my head, and I spent about twenty minutes mapping out who he was. The key for me was to get a feel for his attitude and his voice. If I were taking more than five days to write the novel, I probably would have taken the time to write a mini bio. Nothing too detailed, just enough so that before writing the novel I would have stronger feel for his point of view.

I like my characters to change, even small ones, and after getting to know Nathaniel, I wasn't sure what his arc would be. Not wanting to waste time, I moved forward knowing it was something I would have to work out later.

If you are new to writing, I suggest taking the time now to figure out what flaws your characters have and if they will go through any kind of arc to change for the better or worse. My book *Finish the Script!* has a whole chapter dedicated to character arcs, so if you are struggling, it's a good resource for that.

The more you understand and know who your protagonist is, the easier it will be to write your 5 Day Novel. Don't skimp or take shortcuts during the character creation process because, if you do, you will pay for it later.

Assignment: Create your protagonist.

The Pitch

When I taught college, I required my students to pitch their story ideas before they were allowed to write them. As an instructor, it helped me make sure they were on the right track and weren't aimlessly grasping at nothing.

As I worked with more and more students, I realized that creating a pitch served as an important tool. It helped them shape their core ideas before writing, and if they ever got lost during the writing process, it was a terrific point of reference to help them get back on track.

I have a whole chapter dedicated to writing pitches in *Finish the Script!* I won't go over the whole thing again here. The long and short of it is that, when writing a pitch, you need to include your protagonist, what they want, and what gets in their way. The tone of your story should be clear as well. Breaking down *Ameriguns*, it looks something like this...

- Protagonist: Nathaniel Ryder (FBI Agent)
- Protagonist's Wants: To keep people safe
- Antagonist: Ameriguns, lone wolf gunmen
- Genre: Action Thriller

Looking at that, I saw that Nathaniel's want was pretty vague. It's so generic, and as a character, he should want something more specific. It's fine for an overall pitch in an action genre, but I realized it was time to make a choice about what Nathaniel's arc would be.

I knew whatever journey Nathaniel went through wouldn't be easy. At some point, I would have to kill off people he loved. Either at the very beginning of the novel, at the very end, or in both places.

Few things in life can change a person's personality, but trauma is one of them. I've seen it first hand, and I decided that Nathaniel is a highly empathetic person, and going through the ringer, he would end up broken. At the end of the book, he would decide that field work and trying to climb the ladder in the FBI wouldn't be his thing. Instead he'd shift, avoid the atrocities, and focus on analyst work not field work.

For going into a first draft, the arc wasn't bad. It gave me a direction and tied in well with the theme of gun violence. But I also knew that, like with everything in prewriting, it's not set in stone. If when writing I discovered new or more interesting things about Nathaniel, I could easily adjust the arc.

Feeling a bit more confident on the overall direction with *Ameriguns*, I churned this out as my pitch...

> After surviving a mass shooting, FBI Agent Nathaniel Ryder is forced to confront his worst fears as Ameriguns, a group of lone wolf gunmen, put Washington, D.C., under siege.

I was happy with it, but decided to take it a step further. I've been doing this indie author thing for a while now, and the pitch is so close to being a book blurb that I went for it and wrote the actual description for the book, even though I hadn't written the book yet...

> Lone Wolf Gunmen Terrorize the Nation's Capital!
>
> After witnessing a family member die during a mass shooting, FBI Agent Nathaniel Ryder is forced to confront his worst fears as Ameriguns, a group of lone wolf gunmen, put Washington D.C., under siege.
>
> When Ryder's superiors suspect him of orchestrating the terror, he must go on the run, unable to trust his co-workers or friends. Only he can clear his name and put an end to the killings.

If you love action packed thrillers, you'll love Scott King's *Ameriguns*. Buy it today and let the heart pounding begin!

The opening headline and the bottom call to action are marketing fluff, but that second paragraph was a huge help. It gave me a direction to take in the second half of the novel.

Knowing the novel would have a lot of violence, I understood that I had to space events out so that, as the story progressed, life would get worse and worse for Nathaniel. Generally by the end of Act II, you want your character broken and feeling as if they have been destroyed.

To get a person to that rock bottom state, you can target specific parts of their life. Most people have a work life, a home life, and love life (can also be friendship). By messing up those three aspects of a person's life, you can crush nearly anyone.

It's common in thrillers for a protagonist to be on the run. I liked the idea of having everyone turn against Nathaniel at the end of Act II and leaving him on his own while trying to stop the bad guys.

As silly as it may seem to write a pitch or even a fleshed out book blurb for a novel you've not written yet, I cannot stress enough how useful it is.

Assignment: Write a pitch for your novel. Make sure to include your protagonist, what they want, what is getting in their way, and the genre of your story.

POV and Tense

Knowing the different points of views (POV) and how to use them is important, so let's go over the main kinds: first person, second person, third person limited, and third person omniscient.

First Person uses "I" or "we," and the descriptions are written from one person's perspective, like this...

> *I walked into the coffee shop. The berry Ethiopian blend filled my nostrils as I strutted to the counter to place my order. I pictured my mother's face, the smell of the coffee having reminded me of the herbal tea she used to drink.*

When you write in first person, it gets the reader directly into the POV character's head. It's an open door to their thoughts. When done right   your readers bond with your character a lot faster.

Keep in mind, writing in first person is more than using "I" when describing things. A first person POV yields a story told by the character. So instead of the narration in the author's voice, it is written in the character's voice.

For something like a 5 Day Novel where you have a limited time to get a book done and limited space to make sure your readers connect with your character, going with a first person POV would be a smart choice.

Second person uses "you," and the descriptions are written like this...

You walked into the coffee shop. The berry Ethiopian blend filled your nostrils, reminding you of the herbal tea your mother used to drink.

Writing in second person is strange because it addresses the reader directly. I did it when I wrote *The Eye of Hastur*, a choose your own adventure style book. I had a lot of fun doing it. Outside of interactive fiction, second person is rarely used, and if it is, it's very hard to use right.

Unless you are an experienced author and truly know what you are doing, you are better off avoiding second person.

Third person limited uses "he," "she," and "they," and the descriptions are written like this...

Nathaniel Ryder walked into the coffee shop. The berry Ethiopian blend filled his nostrils. He pictured his mother's face, the smell reminding him of the herbal tea she used to drink.

Outside of first person, third person limited is the most common POV in contemporary writing. In many ways, it is like having a camera that follows your characters around, but instead of seeing the world through their eyes, it is as if the camera sits over their shoulder. You still get a sense of how that character sees the world, and you also can observe their thoughts, but the view isn't as deep as it would be in first person.

The main reason to use third person limited is that, instead of having only one main POV character, you can have a bunch of them. In the epic fantasy novel I just fished, I had six POV characters. This allowed me to spend different chapters with different characters so that the reader gets to bond with all of them and observe more of the world and the story.

It is important when writing in third person limited that you don't head hop, meaning in a single chapter or section, you don't switch from Character A's POV to Character B's POV. Swapping POVs from paragraph to paragraph is more along the lines of third person omniscient.

An example of Third Person Omniscient would be...

The barista with the bible verse tattoos watched as the man entered the coffee shop. He walked with a stilted stride, and the bulge on his hip meant he was carrying. She knew that meant law enforcement.

As Nathaniel strutted to the counter, he breathed in the Ethiopian blend. The smell of it reminded him of the herbal tea his mother used to drink.

Third person omniscient has fallen out of style in modern times, but it is still a valid way to tell a story. It's like writing third person limited but instead of limiting your view to one character's perspective at a time you are allowed to jump around and see multiple perspectives.

If you are writing your novel in third person, you need to make it clear from the start if it is limited or omniscient. Switching between the two will cause reader confusion, and that is bad. You don't want anything in your novel that will pull your reader out of the story. Every time they are pulled out, there is the chance they will decide to not go back into it.

Handling third person omniscient takes skill. I've never done it, but think I could... MAYBE. It's that hard to do right, and when it's done poorly, it is so horribly bad. In many ways third person omniscient is like first person in the sense that you as an author are not telling the story. There is a narrative voice, and that narrator is the one telling the story.

In addition to POVs, you will also need to decide what tense your story should be written in: past tense or present tense?

Past tense example:

Nathaniel strutted to the coffee bar.

Present tense example:

Nathaniel struts to the coffee bar.

Most novels are written in the past tense. But some are written in present because writing in present can give the story more of a sense of immediacy. You will see present tense show up a lot in thrillers or teen novels, and before choosing which POV or tense you will use for your novel you should consider what is common for the genre you are writing in.

I learned to write via screenwriting, and screenplays are written in present tense because when a person watches a movie they see the action unfold in real time on the screen. I love present tense, and I really wanted to write my epic fantasy novel in present tense, but I knew doing so would be a mistake.

Epic fantasies are ancient. The mythos within them can span hundreds or thousands of years. In a straight up epic fantasy, using present tense would feel off. If I were writing a bank heist thriller set in a fantasy world, I could probably get away with present tense, but not a grand epic.

It's common for teen novels to be written in first person because, in general, teenagers are self-focused. Writing in first person allows the readers to jump right into the character's head. Look at novels like *The Fault in Our Stars* or *The Hunger Games*. Both were written in first person and would be completely different books if they had been done in third person limited.

For my 5 Day Novel, it made sense to write the book in first person, but I'm not a fan of writing this POV. I don't like deep POVs, so I settled on third person limited. I was really excited to write *Ameriguns* in present tense and totally meant to. I wrote the first chapter in the present tense, but then somewhere in chapter two, I switched to past tense and didn't realize till chapter four that it had happened. Deciding it was easier to rewrite one chapter instead of three, I stuck with past tense for the novel.

When picking which POV and tense you will use for your novel, make sure you are aware of what is common in the genre and what you are comfortable writing.

Assignment: Choose the POV and tense your novel will be written in.

OUTLINE

I've never believed in writer's block. I think it's poop. Writer's block translates to being stuck with a story and not knowing where to take it. What causes being stuck? Not planning. If you plan out your novel, you will never have to deal with writer's block.

This brings me to the whole pantsers vs. outliners debate. Pantsers like to fly by the seat of their pants and write to see where the story takes them. Outliners are like me and want to know ahead of time where thing are going. Both are valid ways to write.

When I taught college, I required my students to prepare an outline to keep them on track, and if you are doing a 5 Day Novel, I suggest you do the same. Working at such a fast pace leaves little room for errors or fixing problems that evolve from an unplanned story.

Having an outline, even a thin one, can you keep you typing instead of stopping to consider which way to take the story or how you need to go back and set-up a bunch of the new plot points you discovered.

An outline is a map of your story. It's not set in stone. Even when you work from an outline, you will discover new twists and turns as you progress. The outline is there to remind you of where you are going so you can't ever get too far from where you need to be.

Since I was working under pressure, I didn't want to get crazy with how I structured *Ameriguns*. I defaulted to a three act structure, the kind you'd use in a screenplay, but altered it to fit the needs of the story. Because of what I wanted to do with *Ameriguns*, this is where my outline started:

Opening - Nathaniel Ryder survives a mass shooting.

Character stuff - Jump ahead eight to ten months and slow down the story to establish Nathaniel's life. We will get to see him around work, family, and friends.

Catalyst - Ameriguns make their first attack.

Middle Junk - Nathaniel investigates Ameriguns, and the attacks get worse and worse. Eventually his superiors suspect he is the one behind them.

Rock Bottom - Nathaniel is on his own, being hunted by the FBI, and only he can stop the final Ameriguns attack.

Climax - Mirror the opening mass shooting, but this time Nathaniel saves the day.

Epilogue - Nathaniel turns away from field work to become an analyst.

Because of the nature of my story, I stopped working on the outline and had to decide who the villain was and why they did what they were doing.

SPOILER WARNING: This is your last spoiler warning. Don't read any more if you want to read *Ameriguns* unspoiled.

I decided my villains were victims of gun violence and that they were working together to create the worst mass shootings that the US had ever seen. Their goal would be to target politicians, their families, and lifestyles in the hopes that, after suffering these tragic events, Congress might actually move forward to create new gun regulations.

The concept felt pretty bat crazy. Yet the more I thought about it, the more I could see someone trying something so ridiculous. Grief can do terrible things to people, and after researching gun violence and seeing first hand how zealot-like people's passions can appear on both sides of the issue, it didn't seem too much of a stretch.

To make it work, I would need to tie the leader of Ameriguns to Nathaniel. Someone who had appeared in the story earlier so that when the revelation happened at the end of act II, it would crush Nathaniel.

Because I knew I needed to really hurt Nathaniel emotionally, I decided that the novel should open in a mass shooting where Nathaniel's brother is killed. Nathaniel's sister-in-law would be present, and she would serve as the main antagonist in the book.

With the big bad in place, I mapped out the timeline for the middle of the novel. The main events focused on how Ameriguns would try to execute their twisted plan. It was a risky move because basing the structure on the antagonist meant my protagonist would become reactionary. A reactionary protagonist is acceptable, but if done badly they can end up feeling too passive.

I still wasn't sure though what other things should go in the middle of the novel, so I made a giant list of cool stuff I wanted to happen somewhere in the book. Here is a segment of the list...

Flirting, chase scene, police shooting, on the run from the FBI, a dog, family time, armed drone, a politician, gun control laws, Georgetown, a reporter/media type person, the way the media covers gun violence, religion, the National Cathedral, the DC metro, betrayal, not trusting people...

I took all those cool things, merged them with the *Ameriguns* timeline and my basic structure, and formed them into a giant chronological list. Here is the first sequence...

Nathaniel gets a call. His sister-in-law says there is a man with a gun at the wedding they are attending.

Nathaniel runs to the wedding. It's at a park along the Potomac River. On the way he calls 911. The wedding is a massacre. Nathaniel finds his sister-in-law safe and hiding.

Nathaniel tracks down his brother. The shooter has his brother and the groomsmen cornered.

Nathaniel aims to take a kill shot to save his brother... a police sniper shoots Nathaniel. Nathaniel doesn't get to stop the shooter. He watches his brother being killed and is beaten/thrown around by a racist officer.

One important thing to understand about thrillers is that their chapters often end with cliffhangers. Not always huge life or death ones, but ones that propel the reader to keep on reading.

Repeatedly ramping up the drama can get old, and if you haven't included calm moments to allow the reader to stop and take a breath, then the task of reading will feel heavy and exhausting. That meant I should structure my chapters so that they ended in cliffhangers but slowed down just a bit in the middle of the chapters. Or every so often, after big sequences, I had whole chapters that were more reflective.

Taking pacing into account I broke down the first few chapters of *Ameriguns* to look like this:

Chapter 1:
- Nathaniel receives phone call from sister-in-law.
- He runs to wedding massacre while calling 911.
- He tells his sister-in-law over the phone what to do.
- The phone line goes dead with loud banging noise.

Chapter 2:
- Nathaniel finds sister-in-law safe in mobile bathroom-trailer.
- The loud noise turns out to be shooter kicking in men's room door.
- Nathaniel and sister-in-law share a calm moment.

- They hear gunshots fired outside.
- Nathaniel sends sister-in-law away and goes to investigate.

Chapter 3:

- Nathaniel walks through a horrific massacre. It is heartbreaking and tragic.
- Nathaniel tracks the shooter. He has the wedding party cornered, including Nathaniel's brother.
- Nathaniel aims to fire his weapon to take out the shooter.
- A bullet rips through Nathaniel's leg.

Chapter 4

- Nathaniel falls from the bullet wound.
- The shooter kills Nathaniel's brother.
- D.C., SWAT takes out the shooter.
- D.C., SWAT apprehends Nathaniel, and he realizes it was the police who shot him and prevented him from saving his brother.
- The D.C., SWAT realize they screwed up and that Nathaniel is FBI.
- Nathaniel faints from blood loss.

I outlined the entire book like this and ended up with forty-eight chapters. I made sure that the majority of chapters ended on a twist or action moment, but that there were lots of calm spots throughout the whole story in between.

Once I was happy with the outline, I compared it to the pitch and book blurb that I had written. I made sure the tones matched and that I was telling the story I had planned to tell.

If for some reason the outline and pitch didn't match, I could rewrite the pitch to fit the outline or restructure the outline to fit the pitch. Either way works; it just depends upon whether the pitch or outline feels like a better story.

Although I used the three act structure for my outline, there are lots of other ways to write one. You might consider researching the scene-sequel method, the MICE quotient, story maps, or the billion other ways to do it. No matter what you choose, make sure it's a method that excites you and that you feel comfortable using. The method of outlining is the way that works best for you.

Assignment: Outline your novel.

THE FULL CAST

Unless you are writing a story about a protagonist who is isolated from everyone else, you will need to create additional characters to include in your story.

When I'm developing characters, the first two things I do are to get a feel for their attitude and listen to their voice. When deciding who Nathaniel was, I knew right away that he had a big heart. He does what he does because he cares about people and honestly wants to make a difference. The thought of cheating, breaking the law, or doing something dishonest isn't in him. That's not who he is.

With my outline as a guide, I made a list of all the additional characters I needed to create for *Ameriguns*. I knew who my antagonist was, who the supporting cast were, and I even knew where I wanted all the scenes to take place.

The three main people I needed to spend time with were Lori, Jay, and Vargas. Lori is Nathaniel's sister-in-law and the big bad. Jay is Nathaniel's best friend who also happens to be a cable TV news host. Special Agent Bianca Vargas is Nathaniel's direct supervisor at work. The three characters represented Nathaniel's work life, romantic life (friendship counts), and home life, and it was important that each aspect felt alive.

Lori was pretty easy to nail. I pictured her as a yuppy type-a personality. She would be a teacher, and from coping with the loss of her husband will have developed a new friendship/codependency with Nathaniel.

Jay was fun to create. I wanted him to be the host of something like *Last Week Tonight* or *The Daily Show*. I named his show *Today with Jay!* To cheat, I decided the way he talked would be based on myself. I have a weird, sarcastic sense of humor, and making Jay's word choice and sentence structure like my own would make sure he didn't sound at all like Nathaniel.

Vargas took a bit of work. I wanted her gruff and tough, but not in that cliché way that tough female characters can be. I decided that she was a woman who wanted to be good at her job. It was being good that mattered to her and being the best. She's competitive but not the type of character who gives a flying fluff about climbing the ladder at the FBI.

For the supporting cast, I needed a whole slew of characters: multiple politicians, a physical therapist who could serve as a possible love interest for Nathaniel, members of Ameriguns, other FBI agents, and Nathaniel's brother.

With such a short amount of time I made only short notes for the rest of the cast list. Here is an example of that...

> Madelyn Campbell - Senator from Texas. A bit of Texas slang in her speech (hoss & fixing & no bueno), but mostly she's like a Texan version of Emily Gilmore (the grandmother from Gilmore Girls). She's scary, and if you cross her, she will destroy you.

A lot of my notes regarding characters have to do with their voice because, as you know, all characters should talk different. If you cut corners on character creation because of time, make sure you at least have an idea for how each character sounds.

Depending on the kind of story you are telling, the location might also serve as a character. If there is any kind of world building you need to do, now is the time to do it.

I knew my book would be set in Washington, D.C., and in my outline I included Georgetown, the Capitol Building, the J. Edgar Hoover Building, Cathedral of St. Matthew the Apostle, GWU Hospital, Embassy Row, Nationals Park, and a few other places.

I wanted my characters to really live in D.C. Sure the big stuff, like the White House, might be there in the background, but at the same time, I made sure the characters went to the kinds of places where actual locals go, like Lincoln's Waffle Shop or the jogging trail along Rock Creek Park.

A great litmus test for location is asking what would happen if you pulled your story and characters out of your planned setting and put them somewhere else. If the story still works without any problem, chances are your world building needs a bit more work.

Assignment: Flesh out the cast of your novel. Pay extra attention to your antagonist, co-stars, and the setting.

DAY ONE JOURNAL

This is the blog post I wrote in the evening of DAY ONE while writing my 5 Day Novel...

Today was all prewriting...

At the start of the day, I had no game plan for the novel I would be writing this week other than that it would be an action thriller. After staring at computer paper with sketches and strange lists all day, I officially know what I want this book to be.

I wrote my pitch for the book, drafted a rough outline, completed character arcs, created a detailed outline, did some research, crafted a final outline. So I think I'm ready to go tomorrow.

I'm really tempted to share the pitch, but the book is more character focused than a pure action story, and it will touch upon themes that are sensitive. So I don't want to share the details until I get further into it since things may change. I will say that the protagonist is an FBI agent living in Washington, D.C., and there is a mix of politics along with the action.

Tomorrow is going to be the hardest day physically. I'm going to try to get 50k words done or at least the full first draft. That may end up being 44k or 51k. I won't know till I get there. Lisa is requiring that I take breaks to get up and move and still do at least a daily five-mile walk. So that will cut into my writing time. Not sure how many words I can write in a single day, but I guess I will find out tomorrow. I'm hoping I can do at least 2k an hour, which means that I should be able to get a draft done in like twenty to twenty-four hours.

DAY ONE CHECKLIST

- **Assignment:** Form the main idea for your novel.
- **Assignment:** Pick the genre(s) your novel will fall into.
- **Assignment:** Create your protagonist.
- **Assignment:** Write a pitch for your novel. Make sure to include your protagonist, what they want, what is getting in their way, and the genre of your story.
- **Assignment:** Choose the POV and tense your novel will be written in.
- **Assignment:** Outline your novel.
- **Assignment:** Flesh out the cast of your novel. Pay extra attention to your antagonist, co-stars, and the setting.
- **Bonus Assignment:** Start writing your 5 Day Novel!

Day Two: Writing

Day Two Plans

The one goal for DAY TWO is to write. Put your butt in that chair. Put your fingers on the keyboard and don't stop typing.

My hope for DAY TWO was to hit somewhere near 50k words. Spoiler... I didn't. I started writing at 5:00 a.m. and stopped at 10:30 p.m. I hit just over 28,400 words, which is still a lot and awesome, but not what I was shooting to hit.

Jumping into DAY TWO, I couldn't allow any distractions. My focus was on putting words on the page. I did take a few breaks. I stood up, walked around, took the puppies into the backyard, and I did my daily five-mile walk.

If I hadn't taken care of myself by sleeping, exercising, and eating, I wouldn't have had the focus or strength to finish my 5 Day Novel. When you plan your own writing sessions, make sure you include those things.

And although I was disappointed at writing *only* 28k words on DAY TWO, it was still an achievement. Until I attempted the 5 Day Novel, I had never written more than 8k words in a day. Since finishing the challenge and working on this book, I had a day when I wrote 11k and hadn't been meaning to!

No Take Backs

The basic writing advice you see everywhere is that you shouldn't edit when writing. Editing slows your progress and switches your brain from one type of task to another. From my own experience and from watching my students work, the question of if you should edit while writing depends on the writer and their goal.

If you are trying to hit 30k–50k in a single day, then you will have to rein in your inner critic, or you won't get anywhere. For some people it might be easy to do so. For others it will be a grueling task.

The inner critic is a pain, but it serves an important role, especially when it comes time to perform heavier rewrites and line edit. The problem is that, when trying to write a novel at such a fast pace, you don't have time to listen to the critic. You're better off ignoring it and moving forward no matter what the cost.

There are few writers who can pull off doing a publishable first draft. Dean Koontz is the only famous author I know of the top of my head who can do so. Even so, he has said he will sometimes do thirty to forty drafts of a single page before moving on to the next.

That means a good 99 percent of authors write unpublishable first drafts. Once you accept and understand that it's alright if your first draft sucks, it's easier to silence your inner editor.

In the '80s and '90s, there were certain unspoken rules on the playground. One of the biggest was "no take backs." Basically, that means if you give someone something, you aren't allowed to take it back. It's officially theirs.

The only way to crank out tens of thousands of words in a single day is with a "no take back" mentality. No matter what you put on the page, keep moving forward. You aren't allowed to take the words back.

Assignment: Don't allow yourself to edit while writing.

No Distractions

We live in age of notifications. We have a constant connection to the outside world, which means we have constant distractions, things that pull us away from our writing.

Life responsibilities, like paying the bills, taking care of kids, and those things happen. You plan and work around them the best you can. But other distractions, like social media and the rest of the internet, are ones you can control.

When doing my 5 Day Novel, I went old school and unplugged our router. Having my computer disconnected meant I couldn't get online. I could have done the same thing with my phone by turning it off or by putting it in airplane mode, but I didn't. I was bad in that manner. Don't be like me. Do everything in your power to cut online distractions.

I left my phone on because I'm a very visual person, and there were times when I wanted to go into Google Maps and check out the street view of locations in Washington, D.C. I used it as a refresher to remember the sights, sounds, smells. For the most part, it worked. It didn't work on DAY THREE.

On DAY THREE, I fell into a research hole. Research holes are dangerous, and they happen so innocently. I picked up my phone with the intention of Googling one quick thing. I wanted to find out the difference between a cream color and an eggshell color. Forty minutes later, I was randomly trying to piece together information about a Saudi Arabian prince from the 1980s.

We are all different, and there is no telling what your Achilles heel might be. Maybe you are a sucker for cat photos, unboxing videos, or trying to track down the mystery of Mount Weather and Raven Rock Mountain. The thing to remember is that distractions are dangerous, and unless you are like Sam Gamgee with a will of steel, something will tempt you away from writing. The best way around that is to cut all internet ties while doing the first draft. If you need to look something up or research that's fine, but mark your spot and do it later.

Assignment: Cut online distractions so you don't fall down research holes nor get bogged down by social media.

SAFE ZONE

Brew-n-Bake, the local coffee shop here in Lake Jackson is my safe zone. It's where I go to avoid distractions. I'm sitting at my corner table right now as I type this.

As much as I love Brew-n-Bake, I didn't write my 5 Day Novel there. I couldn't afford to waste the time it took to drive there and back again. I had to make sure every minute of my week counted. That meant I needed to make a new distraction-free zone at home.

I have a home office. Along one wall is an eight foot desk where I have my computer. To both sides of it are book shelves, and around the other three walls are more book shelves. It's a nice office and works great when I need to process photos and work on marketing or publishing.

For writing, my office is a huge distraction. There is a stack of to-be-read books I keep on the corner of my desk, and I have a small bin of to-do items. Plus, if I'm at home, it means there is laundry to do, dishes to wash, or a stack of board games that I need to photograph for clients.

To get our house and my office in shape for doing the 5 Day Novel, I went on a cleaning binge the Sunday before I started. I made sure there was no clutter and left nothing on my desk except for my computer. I dusted the house, vacuumed, cleaned toilets, and made sure everything was as tidy as possible.

I also cleared out all the dog and cat toys from the office and moved the cat tent and tunnel to the living room. It's not that I don't love my furry babies, it's just that they can be needy, and I wanted to trim down interruptions from them.

Getting my house together was important for me in making the office a safe zone where I wouldn't be distracted. As I've said before, I'm a weird duck. Your mileage may vary. Creating a safe zone for you might be setting up a laptop in a guest room. It might mean swapping out your yellow light bulbs for white daylight balanced bulbs. As humans, we all have quirks. You should know yourself well enough to determine what might distract you. Whatever those things might be, deal with them.

Beyond the physical space, I did several other things to get our house ready for the challenge. One of which was to make a playlist that I could listen to when writing.

Whenever I start a new project, I create a playlist for it.

Back in the day when I wrote screenplays, I could use words with lyrics. If I was working on something angsty, I might play some pop music, or if there was a lot of action, the music I chose would have a faster pace.

As I started writing novels, I fell out of using music with words. It was too brain bending. Now I listen to musical scores. Since a lot of what I write is fantasy based, I've found myself drawn to the sound tracks of the Studio Ghibli movies or even video game soundtracks.

For writing *Ameriguns*, I bought the soundtracks to season one and two of *Daredevil*, the soundtrack for *Jessica Jones*, and a bootleg version of the soundtrack for *Stranger Things* I ripped from YouTube 'cause the real thing wasn't out yet. As I'm writing *The 5 Day Novel*, I'm listening to a bought copy of the first volume of *Stranger Things* and am very excited about the second, which comes out this Friday!

Music helps me get into the right head space for a story. It helps me feel the tone and genre that I want to convey. If you've never tried creating a soundtrack for a novel, I suggest giving it a go.

The final thing I did to lessen distractions during the 5 Day Novel challenge was precook meals. On the same Sunday when I did all the cleaning, I also did a bunch of cooking. I'm the default chef in our house 'cause Lisa isn't a good cook. To make it easier on both of us, I prepped the meals and froze them. That way I could make a dash to the fridge and microwave and be back to writing in minutes.

Getting our house together, preparing the music playlist, and making sure I didn't need to waste time cooking were all part of making a safe zone so that I could focus solely on writing, and without having done so, there is no way I could have finished *Ameriguns* in the allotted five days.

Assignment: Make sure your distraction-free safe zone is ready so that you can write your 5 Day Novel.

BREAKS & FOOD

Blood clots are gross and scary. They develop in veins deep below your skin, and the longer you sit in one position, the greater your chance of developing one. Once a blood clot forms, it can get knocked free, and when that happens it might end up in your heart, brain, lungs, or somewhere else just as bad. That means doing something crazy, like writing a novel in five days, can kill you if you don't take care of yourself.

Online advice for preventing deep vein thrombosis (DVT), the technical term for blood clots, is not always consistent. Some sources suggest getting up and moving every two hours. Other say you need to do it every ninety minutes, while some contend that not getting up is fine as long as you do leg curls, pumps, and lifts while sitting.

I'm not a physician, and this is not medical advice, so you should do your own research. What I did when doing my 5 Day Challenge was get up every seventy-five minutes. I had an alarm set, and when it went off, I stood up and got fresh coffee from the kitchen, or took the dogs out, or did some other thing. I also exercised every day, doing a five-mile walk that took about seventy-five minutes to do.

I won't lie. It was a pain in the butt. I grew to hate that flipping alarm, and I wish I could get back the time I spent doing walks because it's time I could have been writing.

On DAY TWO, the walk was brutal 'cause all I wanted to do was type, but on DAY FOUR and DAY FIVE, I appreciated the time away from the computer. It was a chance for me to gain perspective and work out any problems I had encountered.

At the end of the day, our bodies are machines, and I think taking breaks and doing the daily walk helped keep me healthy so that I could write. Sleep was just as important. Generally, I'm good for six and a half hours of sleep but can still function as long as I get five hours. If I get fewer than five, my brain ends up broke, and I can't write.

Our brains are muscles in this way, and I tried to treat the five-day challenge as if it were a sporting event. To stay energized, I snacked on popcorn, nuts, fresh fruit, and veggies with homemade hummus. I also ate full, balanced meals at set times.

As with our writing methods, our bodies are different. We all have distinct health needs. If you want to do a 5 Day Novel, determine what your needs are and make sure you can meet them easily. Doing so will allow you to function at peak performance levels.

Assignment: Make sure that exercise, breaks, snacks, and meals are a part of your preparation for writing a 5 Day Novel.

Write Now

If you are going to do a 5 Day Novel, you need to understand the commitment it takes to sit and type nonstop. You also need to know that only you can make yourself do it. I can't stand behind you and slap you with a yardstick every time you get distracted. Only you can make sure that you keep on typing.

With everything else out of the way, you should be able to spend almost all DAY TWO writing. Going into the challenge, I thought I could maintain between 2,000 and 3,000 words per hour. At that rate, it would take me eighteen to twenty-four hours to write a 50k word novel.

As DAY TWO blurred by, I realized I wasn't going to be able to finish the first draft in a single day. I seemed to be averaging 1,500 words per hour at most.

I got so desperate that, as the story moved along, I tried to take shortcuts to get myself further into the draft. Here is a sample paragraph from my first draft of *Ameriguns*. I'm going to tell my editor not to edit it and leave it exactly as is...

LEG HURTS SAVING PEOPLE

Going room by room he checked for patients. When Nathaniel found one he could help, he got them to thier feet and into the hall.

He wasn't the only one not running. Several docotrs and nurses were doing the same thing. **FLESH THIS WHOLE SCENE OUT WITH DIALOG AND ACTION. MOOR DESCRIPTIVE WITH PATIENS SO WE CARE.**

Those are the actual typos and formatting. It was a total cheat, and by doing it, I only made more work for myself that would have to be addressed during rewrites.

Some places were fine to cheat. I had a scene of dialog in a car, and I knew that the characters would be driving through Dupont Circle and that region of D.C. While doing the first draft, I wanted only to focus on the spoken words and blocking of the characters. So instead of having descriptions of the neighborhood, which were important and story related, I left a note at the top of the scene. "Yo, when you come back, make sure you add scenery and set up the buildings for the climax."

The first kind of cheating was wrong because it was lazy writing. I didn't want to have to think about the scene or deal with it. The second kind of cheat was fine because I was still writing a full scene. I just focused on one part of it, knowing I'd flesh the rest out later.

Even with cheating, I got only about two-thirds of the way through my outline before having to call it quits on DAY TWO. There is a physical limit on how much a person can write a day, and I hit mine near the 28k range.

For sure, my dyslexia affected my writing speed. I can't count the number of times I wrote "National" instead of "Nathaniel." Seriously, when doing rewrites, it was so bad that "National" was one of my most used words in the whole novel. Even if the dyslexia hadn't slowed me down, I don't think I could have done more than 30k–35k words at an extreme max.

If I were to do the 5 Day Novel again, I would have started writing on DAY ONE, and instead of planning to finish a full draft in a single day, I would have broken it up into three days. As it played out, by the end of DAY TWO I was mentally spent. My words were slurred, my eyes burned, and I had nothing left in me.

I was so upset at failing to finish the first draft in a single day that I thought about scrapping the whole concept. I really wanted to call it quits. I would say I failed. I'd sleep, and instead of finishing the book in the next three days like I had planned, I'd take a full week to two weeks.

If I hadn't posted about the 5 Day Novel online, I think I

would have thrown in the towel. The only thing that kept me going at the end of DAY TWO were the people cheering for me. I had made the challenge public, and with it came a sense of accountability, so instead of quitting, I sucked it up and went to bed knowing I'd jump back in on DAY THREE.

Assignment: Start or continue writing your first draft and write as much as you can without hurting yourself.

DAY TWO JOURNAL

This is the blog post I wrote in the evening of DAY TWO while writing my 5 Day Novel…

I REALLY wanted to get 50k words done today. That didn't happen. Apparently there is a physical limit of words a person can type in a day. You can only type X amount of words per hour, and I just didn't keep up the speed I needed.

In twelve hours, I hit 18,080 words. I'm feeling pretty beat and haven't even hit the halfway point. I'm going to take a break for dinner and then jump back in. If I push, I think I can hit 24k–26k total for the day. That's planning for a bedtime around 11:00 p.m.

Although today's numbers aren't what I was hoping them to be, it does mean I should be able to hit 45–50k tomorrow and finish the first draft. I had planned for tomorrow to be a half day of writing and a half day of rewriting, but that's impossible now.

It's ok. I can still do this five-day challenge. It just means Thursday will have to be all rewrites, and then Friday I'll focus on getting the polish done. Phew I'm feeling fried though. This fast pass process is not something I could keep up on a normal basis. It's both physically and mentally draining and, thus, not sustainable.

DAY TWO CHECKLIST

- **Assignment:** Don't allow yourself to edit while writing.
- **Assignment:** Make sure you take breaks to move around and exercise.
- **Assignment:** Make sure you eat and drink right to stay healthy and energized.
- **Assignment:** Cut online distractions so you don't fall down research holes nor get bogged down by social media.
- **Assignment:** Make sure your distraction-free safe zone is ready so that you can write your 5 Day Novel.
- **Assignment:** Make sure that exercise, breaks, snacks, and meals are a part of your preparation for writing a 5 Day Novel.
- **Assignment:** Start or continue writing your first draft and write as much as you can without hurting yourself.

Day Three: More Writing

DAY THREE PLANS

DAY THREE is about finishing your first draft, and if you get ahead, starting the rewrite.

As defeated as I felt when going to bed on DAY TWO, I woke up feeling better on DAY THREE. In fact, instead of jumping in and writing the second I woke up, I ate breakfast with Lisa and enjoyed the time with her.

I knew if I could handle 28k words in a single day, then another 12k–17k to finish the draft would be a breeze. With newfound energy, I tore through last third of the book. Not without problems, though. Things come up when you write, and as much as you might plot for them, there are some things you simply cannot plan for.

You are probably smarter than me, which means you didn't wait till DAY TWO to start your first draft. You should be far closer to finishing it than I was at the start of DAY THREE, and if so, all you need to do is power through it and get it done.

Listen to Characters

Remember my very first outline for the structure of *Ameriguns*? In it I had a bit called "middle stuff." The middle of a story is often the hardest part to write. The beginning is all setup. The end is all payoff. The middle is where it's easy to get lost.

That's why we write the outlines. The outlines are supposed to protect us from getting off track, right? Yes and no.

No matter how well you plan, your story will shift and change as you begin to write it. That's not your fault. It's what happens when you breathe life into characters. Regardless of where you want and intend the story to go, sometimes the characters won't listen.

When you hit those roadblocks where it is your will against a character, you need to listen to the character. You may desire that they do X so that Y can happen—badly—but sometimes they just want to do Q instead. If that happens, and it will, go with it.

If characters are making choices on their own, it means you've given them a voice and heart. It's a good sign. If you force a character to do something against their will, the story will feel off. The dialog, scene, and everything tied to it will feel inauthentic to the reader.

When slogging through *Ameriguns,* I hit that problem a few times. The biggest challenge occurred with Senator Madelyn Campbell. She was originally in the story as a bit of a red herring and was meant to be a background character so I could highlight how the media treats gun violence. She was supposed to show up in only three scenes.

No matter how much I tried to keep her away, she kept showing up! Even though I hadn't planned for it or outlined it, she would involve herself with what was going on in the main story to manipulate and move things for her own agenda.

It got so bad that I had to either completely rework the character so she fit my needs or listen to her and adjust my outline to meet *her* needs. I decided to change my plans, and if I hadn't, *Ameriguns* would have been worse off for it because she became one of the most interesting characters in the book.

As you move through the middle and end of your first draft, don't be scared to listen to the characters. They aren't there to sabotage you.

Assignment: Listen to your characters.

SKIP SMALL PROBLEMS

When you start to go off-outline by listening to characters, it can cause a domino effect. A scene that was supposed to happen one way could destroy multiple scenes that were supposed to happen before or after it.

If that happens, you need to decide up front if it is a small problem that needs to be addressed or a big problem. If it's a small problem, don't worry about it and keep moving forward. So much about doing a 5 Day Novel is fighting the clock. It's why you are not supposed to edit as you write and why you have to type so quickly. Time will run out if you don't push hard. Fixing every small problem would become a hinderance.

I had intended to write *Ameriguns* in present tense. As I mentioned earlier, I wrote the very first chapter that way, but then

I screwed up, and the rest of the chapters weren't. I didn't go back and fix the first chapter until I finished my first draft. Why? Because it was a small problem.

A different tense in that one chapter didn't break my story. It needed to be fixed, but wasn't a high priority. If I had gone back and addressed it, I would have ended up reworking dialog, descriptions, and doing a full line edit. It would have been a major speed bump. Instead, I made a mental note and kept moving forward.

Small problems come in all shapes or forms. Maybe I had two characters that started off as siblings and became cousins? Or maybe I have a scene where a character made a phone call, but two scenes earlier they had lost their phone? Instead of going back to fix minor problems, your time is better spent making a mental note and to keep moving forward.

Here are the simple steps for dealing with a minor problem:

1) Decide you have a minor (as opposed to major) problem.

2) Decide what needs to happen to fix the problem.

3) Keep moving forward and finish your first draft, continuing the story as if you had already fixed the problem.

4) When doing rewrites, implement any changes you need to make for earlier scenes.

Assignment: Don't let small problems slow you down.

Deal with Big Problems

As your story evolves, the plot and characters might go more off-outline. And if this creates a major change in your story, then you might have to stop and really address it.

I had one big problem when doing *Ameriguns*. My plan was for the bulk of the book to be set in the spring. This way, a huge plot event could happen at a Nationals' baseball game.

That didn't happen. I blame my dog Winchell. He loves Christmas music, and more specifically, he loves when I sing Christmas music. So even though I did my 5 Day Novel in the heat of the Texas summer, on the morning of DAY TWO right before I started the first draft, I played some Christmas music and sang to him.

It got me in a wintery mood, and it dawned on me that I

could set my novel in the winter! I've not seen snow for three years, before we moved to Texas. The idea of having *Ameriguns* set in D.C., in the winter sounded amazing. I could have snow, winter coats, hot drinks, and all the awesome stuff I missed from home.

I went for it! I set the book in winter. I made New Years relevant to the story. I checked Congress's schedule to see what days they are often in session, and I completely forgot that a scene was supposed to take place at the Nationals' stadium.

On DAY THREE, when I got to the scene that was supposed to happen at the stadium, I cussed and threw my hands up in the air. The whole sequence didn't work without baseball, and I had to stop what I was doing and figure out how to deal with it.

There were two main options: change the time of year, which would mean a lot of rewriting, or change my plans and have the scenes set somewhere equivalent to the Nationals' stadium.

I checked game dates and saw that the Washington Wizards and the Redskins normally play on January 1. I didn't really want to go with the Redskins. There is a lot of drama about the team's name, and I didn't want to put them in the book, in part, because if they do ever change their name, it will date the novel.

I've never been to a Wizard's game (I saw the Bullets who preceded them while growing up), but I have attended concerts at the Verizon Center where the Wizards play.

The Verizon Center was within blocks of three other

locations I had already included. It's in Chinatown, and I've always liked D.C.'s Chinatown. Plus a Metro station sits underneath it, but as much as I wanted to weave D.C.'s subway, I hadn't fit it into my outline.

Although it was not what I had planned, and I had to alter the details and events of the scenes, changing the location to the Verizon Center really worked out in my favor. I needed to address baseball references two scenes earlier in the novel to set things up for the change. I went to the scenes and left myself big bold notes. Then I jumped back to where I had stopped writing and continued my first draft. If your story breaks because of a silly thing you did or because a character did something they wanted, that's alright, and it's not the end of the world. You can survive it!

Here are the simple steps for dealing with a major problem:

1) Decide you have a problem.

2) Decide what needs to happen to fix the problem.

3) Go back to earlier scenes and leave a note in bold reminding yourself of changes you need to make. Don't make those changes now.

4) Keep moving forward and finish your first draft, continuing the story as if you had already fixed the problem.

5) When doing rewrites, watch for those bold notes and fix those scenes then.

Assignment: Stay calm and deal with any big problems.

Don't Get Lost

As you make more changes because of plot holes, writing errors, bad choices, or from listening to characters (or your dog), your novel will become something more than you ever intended it to.

When facing large problems where the story breaks or goes completely off-outline, it is easy to get lost. I've felt it myself, and I've seen it with students. Sometimes as a writer, you don't feel like you are the one in control. The story does what it wants, and you don't see a way to get it back on track.

In those moments you need to remind yourself why this is a story you wanted to write. Go back and reread your pitch. What was the essence of the initial story concept?

My ending for *Ameriguns* changed from what I had thought it was going to be in the outline. The climax was an intimate scene between two characters and ended with one of the characters being killed. I wrote it. The scene worked as a stand alone unit, but it felt off. It felt unsatisfying and didn't convey the message that I wanted it to send.

Feeling exhausted and burned out, I wasn't sure how to fix it. So I took a deep breath, abandoned my office, and decided to do my daily five-mile walk.

Getting away helped to clear my mind, and one of the first things I did to figure out what was wrong with the scene was read my pitch and skim the first chapter.

Ameriguns was always supposed to be action heavy, but that's not how the first draft turned out. With Senator Madelyn Campbell's promotion from background character to one of the more important characters, the novel leaned more toward being a political thriller.

There's nothing wrong with political thrillers, except that both my pitch and the first chapter set-up created reader expectation that there would be lots of action. That's what I had noticed missing in my climax. The intimate scene was fine, but it needed to be followed or preceded by some action.

If you are feeling lost and don't know how to handle the problem or get back on track, turn back to your pitch and ask yourself why you are writing this story.

Assignment: Finish your first draft.

DAY THREE JOURNAL

This is the blog post I wrote in the evening of DAY THREE while writing my 5 Day Novel...

Today was all bout finishing the first draft...

I got to typing at 5:00 a.m. and didn't stop till 11:45. At that point, I ate lunch and jumped back in. Things went well till around 3:00. I took a break to do my daily five-mile walk, showered, and had a thirty minute phone call with my favorite audiobook narrator. Once I got back to my office, things kind of meandered...

I fell down a research hole by accident when I should have been typing, but in doing so, I discovered that in 1989, when I was seven or eight, I met a Saudi Arabian prince in Washington D.C.'s Chinatown. My grandmother took me to a Saudi Arabia exhibit at the convention center. After seeing it and a badass laser show, we went to lunch with the prince. I remember the exhibit in detail, but I have no idea why we went out to lunch with him.

Granny was big into teaching and education. She received a bunch of awards, grants, and met President Reagan, I think twice. My grandfather owned a restaurant and bar near the White House, which always had congressmen and other bigwigs. As a result, I met a lot of people as a kid and never knew why. All I specifically remember about the Saudi Arabian prince (whom I didn't know till today was a prince) was that he called me a "strange boy" because I ordered escargot with a side of french fries and then put vinegar on the fries.

So yeah, weird research hole.

Once I got back to writing, I managed to finish the

first draft of my novel. It's sitting at 38,577 words. That's fine. I'm an underwriter. I know when I do rewrites and the polish that the book will easily grow by 10k–15k. There are a multiple sections where I have things like "DESCRIBE WHAT SHE LOOKS LIKE" and "FIGHT WITH PROTAG GETTING BUTT KICKED." So the book will only expand from where it is now.

Tonight I'm going to make a list of changes that I need to address in the plot and characters. Tomorrow I'm going to start on chapter one and work my way through to the end. I can't believe the week is more than half over. There is still soooooooo much I need to do. Fixing character voices, checking emotions in scenes, making sure I'm happy with the depth of the POV. Uhhhhhh I'm really worried about running out of time!

DAY THREE CHECKLIST

- **Assignment:** Listen to your characters.
- **Assignment:** Don't let small problems slow you down.
- **Assignment:** Stay calm and deal with any big problems.
- **Assignment:** Finish your first draft.
- **Bonus Assignment:** If you get it done at a reasonable hour, start working on DAY FOUR!

Day Four: Rewriting

Day Four Plans

DAY FOUR is all about taking the pile of poop that you excreted all over the pages and adjusting it so that it takes the shape of a concise, understandable story. You do this by rewriting and making multiple passes to fix individual parts and make the whole better.

When planing out the 5 Day Novel challenge, it was super important that I saved enough time to rewrite. Cranking out a first draft is impressive, but so much changes when you write a first draft. In many ways, the first draft is a discovery mission where you as the author are trying to find the story and figure out the characters.

Now that you know who your characters are, you have an understanding of their voices, and you know the exact story you want to tell, it's time to tweak, shift, adjust, and rewrite to make sure everything from page one on up fits into your new understanding.

Diagnosing Problems

It's not easy knowing what about your story sucks. The closer you are to it, the more blurry it gets, and it becomes even more difficult to judge it.

It's why a lot of people suggest that when you finish a novel you should lock it in a drawer and not look at it for three to six months because time away from it will give you distance and allow you to pick it up again without your clouded perception.

When doing a 5 Day Novel, there isn't time to lock your novel in a drawer, which means that, as a writer, you have to be able to diagnose your story and see what isn't working.

We all have flaws when it comes to our writing. As you get to know your voice, you'll get to know where you are weak. As I stated earlier, I'm a horrible underwriter. That means a lot of my rewrite is dealing with the narrative prose to add in more POV, clearer descriptions that appeal to the sense, and those kinds of things.

It is impossible for me to know exactly what your faults are as a writer or what might not be working with your novel, but I at least want to go over the most common things I've seen go wrong in my student's work.

Plot Holes - These are anything in the novel that breaks the story. Events, dialog, or whatever that doesn't add up and hasn't been properly set up.

Weak Characters - These are characters who seem to exist only for the sake of the story. They do not have their own wants or needs outside of the main plot.

Passive Characters - These are characters that go along with the plot and don't make active choices.

Generic Character Voices - This happens when your characters sound too much alike and don't have unique voices.

Too Much/Not Enough Descriptions - When you your narrative prose is too descriptive or doesn't have enough. The later can bog down the story and the former can leave readers confused.

Lack of Clarity in Descriptions - As an author, you know what you mean when you write something. Sometimes, even when you know what you intend, the meaning of those words isn't clear.

Misuse of POV - This can happen from breaking the POV you've established, using a POV that's too deep, or one that's not deep enough.

Pace is Off - This happens when your story moves too fast or too slow. If it's moving too fast, you generally need to add moments where the characters have time to reflect on what's happening. If it's moving too slow, you probably don't have enough conflict.

Lack of Conflict and Drama - This happens when everything is happy, and nothing seems wrong. Conflict doesn't have to be life and death or a big fight. It could be something as simple as someone is thirsty but doesn't have anything to drink. Most scenes should have some form of external or internal conflict.

Tone Is Off - Tone is tied to your voice as an author. If you are still grasping to find your voice, there is a good chance that the tone and transitions between different tones isn't as smooth as it should be.

When diagnosing your novel, treat it like an inverted pyramid. Always start with the big problems and work your way down to the small ones. You want to start big because fixing a large problem could alter the novel. It would suck if you cleaned up and addressed all the small stuff then moved onto something big and discovered you'd have to scrap a lot of the work you'd just done.

For most writers coming off a first draft, the big problems are those that break the plot. During the writing, you will probably have come across at least a few of these and left yourself notes on how you want to address them. Now that you have finished the first draft, it's those kind of breaks that you need to deal with first. (I'll tell you how to do that in the next chapter.)

The next most crucial task to deal with is making sure that all the characters work. Check their wants and needs to make sure that they feel like they exist outside of the plot. Then double check that their voices are unique so that they don't all sound alike. (I'll tell you how to do this as well.)

Once you have a lock on the plot and characters, you can deal with the rest of the problems in the order you feel is best.

Assignment: Make a list of all the problems in your novel and how you will address them.

FIXING THE PLOT

Fixing the plot is normally the easiest problem to tackle. Remember back on DAY THREE when we talked about big and small changes? Most of fixing the plot is going through your draft and making sure all those things are fixed.

It's more than that though. As you read, you should also reevaluate your structure. Whether you used a story grid, MICE Quotient, or the three act structure to craft the plot, double check it and make sure that your execution of the story still fits the structure you chose.

When writing *Ameriguns*, I used a basic three act structure, and for the most part, the final novel reflects that. The big plot problem was that the very end of the book changed from what I had planned. I had envisioned the end of the book being very superhero-ish with Nathaniel rushing off to save innocents from the villain. What happened is that he stopped the big bad, but that wasn't the final climax as written. Instead, in the final moments, the readers are left wondering not if Nathaniel will be a hero, but whether he'll live.

In the scene, Nathaniel is active. He's ridden an emotional roller coaster, and the events thematically work with everything I was trying to touch upon in the novel. The problem is that it wasn't set up that way. To make the moment really pay off, I decided it needed to mirror the opening of the book when Nathaniel is shot by the police, setting it up so that the police would be there again at the end of the climax.

When determining how to fix your plot problems, it might help to reevaluate why you are writing the story you are writing. The message you are trying to send doesn't have to be deep like the one I dealt with in *Ameriguns*, but you do need to ensure that the story makes the point you intend. If it doesn't, you can adjust the plot to make it clearer.

Writing is powerful. As an author, the words you put on a page have the potential to fundamentally change the way someone thinks. Don't let that go to waste because a broken plot muddles your point.

Assignment: Fix the big holes in your plot and make sure the theme and message you are trying to get across comes through loud and clear.

FIXING CHARACTERS

.

Once you've gotten the story locked down, take a hard look at your protagonist. If you wrote a character arc, double check that it adds up and makes sense. When talking about novels, your protagonist doesn't always have to have an arc, so don't feel pressured if you are writing in a genre or a serial where that isn't as common. If you do have one though, make sure all the pieces for it add up.

From there, do the same with your supporting cast members, making sure that their individual stories and plot lines add up and make sense. You particularly want to keep an eye out for any places where you as the author forced the character to do something they didn't want to. If you took a shortcut, now is the time to fix those kinds of problems.

When doing the first draft of *Ameriguns*, I created a character that I didn't know was going to be in the book. Her name is Beasily. She's an FBI agent, and she came about because I needed someone at the FBI who was an equal to Nathaniel, someone who was the same rank and not a special agent or the big boss.

In the two minutes it took to put her on page, I decided she had a big build but is not unhealthy. I also made her a bit on the geeky side. Other than that, I didn't give any thought to her character creation. So when it came time to do rewrites, she needed a lot of work.

Ameriguns is written from Nathaniel's POV. In his head, he has clear desires and goals. To fix Beasily, I had to pretend she was the protagonist of her own story within these events. When she's not in scenes with Nathaniel, what does she want? What does she like?

Originally Nathaniel's arc was about him wanting to be in the field more. FBI field agents rarely work in the field, and if they do, it happens under the supervision of a special agent. But that whole arc kind of got dropped. It turns out that Nathaniel's journey is much more about grief and coping with his brother's death.

I know it was cheating, but I decided to use this scrapped arc for Beasily. I decided she's someone who hungers to be a special agent. She wants it, and she wants it badly. So when things hit the fan toward the end of the novel, it's shocking to her. She comes to discover that what she wanted isn't what she thought it would be. The whole thing works really well, and it makes Beasily one of the most likable and relatable characters in *Ameriguns*.

If you are struggling to fix a character, try what I did with Beasily. Start by establishing their wants and needs and flesh them out from there. What is their existence like outside of the scenes with the protagonist? What things are they passionate about? Do they have things they are passionate about?

No matter if you are trying to fix a problem with a supporting cast member or main character, one of the most common things that can go wrong is that the character acts *out of character*. You spend pages upon pages establishing someone, but then you get to a pivotal scene, and instead of acting one way, which would make sense based on who they are, they act the opposite way because, as the author, you need them to do that one thing for the sake of the plot.

Problems of this kind are easier to fix in the moment. The simplest way to address them is to make sure you listen to your characters when you're in the writing process. If you are on rewrites, it's too late for that, so start trying to think outside the box. In this stage of writing, as the author, you are more about problem solving.

I know of two main ways to correct character inconsistency. First, you can reestablish the character so that the choice they make for the sake of the plot fits who they are. If you don't want to change the character and who they are in all the scenes leading up to that critical moment, then you need to be creative and figure out how you can get what you want while allowing the character to be who they are.

In *Ameriguns*, Special Agent Vargas is dating a US Senator. This fact is revealed near the end of act II, and up until that point, it appeared that something fishy was going on in her life. I did it so that the readers might think she was the big bad.

When it came time to write the reveal scene, I had a problem. The way I outlined made the reveal a huge, scandalous thing. However, as I thought about it, that didn't make sense. Vargas and the Senator were both adults. Neither were married. There was nothing wrong with the two of them dating, other than the fact that they were being discreet.

Being a strong character, Vargas wasn't ashamed of her actions because she had done nothing wrong. At the same time, she wasn't about to let anyone shame her for simply having an adult relationship. That meant what I had thought would be a scandal became a power play between Vargas and Nathaniel.

I really liked it how it turned out, and it went against the normal way a character like her might be shamed. But it caused some plot problems because the scene didn't end the way it was supposed to. It was supposed to end with her convincing Nathaniel she was a good person and not the bad guy. To fix it, I had to change the scene by flipping it. Instead of Vargas trying to prove herself to Nathaniel, Nathaniel had to prove himself to her.

Being true to the characters you have created is the best way to allow them to feel organic and authentic. If you force characters into a mold just because plot demands it, the readers will notice. When in doubt, meet the characters' needs over the plot.

Assignment: Fix any character problems that find after evaluating the story.

CLEANING UP DIALOG

I love dialog. I love writing dialog. Tweaking dialog for me generally results in cutting it. That may be the same for you or the opposite. It just depends on how you write.

With the plot locked and the character problems having been addressed, you can move on to doing a pass where you focus exclusively on the dialog. The cool part about checking the dialog now is that having everything else in place means you really know who your characters are.

It's like in real life when you hang out with someone for a while, you start to guess what they will say. At this stage, you should be able to look back at the earlier parts of your novel and realize that the character voices weren't as clear as they became by the end of the novel.

One of the few problems I had with dialog in *Ameriguns* is that there ended up being a lot more cussing and swearing than I had intended. It's fine that there was cussing. The topics and themes in the book make it appropriate. However, there was so much cussing that it started to make the character voices sound too similar.

To deal with this, I decided to trim back how much my main character cussed. Nathaniel still cusses in the book, but I allow it only when it is important to reveal or draw attention to something.

That being said, I let Jay, the cable TV host, cuss as much as he wanted. He got free rein. It makes sense for his character, and once I started to dial back the other cussing, it helped his voice stand out bit more.

Vargas is my other big cusser in the book. I didn't want to cut her back, so I twisted it. Instead of saying "shit" she says something like "shit nuggets" or instead of saying "fuck" she says "fuck licker." By making the style of how she cussed feel more original, it added more to her voice while distinguishing hers from the other voices.

As silly as cussing is, it works as a great example how to adjust dialog to give characters specific voices. If you notice that all your characters start their dialog with things like "yeah" or "well" or "uh," you can adjust them so that only certain characters speak that way. Doing so will help vary your dialog.

Here is an example...

"Yeah, well, she is tall! Taller than your mom." Jay grinned, as if that proved his point.

"Well, that's not funny," Nathaniel said.

The "yeah" and "well" make the voices sound a bit alike. By cutting one or both of them will help Jay and Nathaniel sound different.

"She is tall! Taller than your mom." Jay grinned, as if that proved his point.

"Not funny," Nathaniel said.

If in the scene I wanted it to sound like Jay was stalling or dragging his feet, I might not have cut the "yea, well." Or if that's how he always talked, I wouldn't have cut it, but as it was, the words were fluffy filler words. They didn't serve a purpose. If you find that several of your characters sound the same, look for those kind of words and play around with their usage to give characters a more distinct voice.

Assignment: Make a dialog pass on your novel, cleaning it up and fixing character voices.

FLESHING OUT POV

Point of view, whether first person or third, affects the narrative prose in a novel. How characters see the world should dictate the descriptions you use as an author. For example, Nathaniel is trained a trained FBI agent. If he walked into a room, he would see it differently than I, Scott King, would see it. Right now, I'm sitting at a table in Brew-n-Bake. If I were to describe the coffee shop as Scott King it might be something like this…

> *"Wood columns and soft earth tones give Brew-n-Bake a calm homey feel. The tables are worn wood, like a bench that has sat outside for years to acquire that thick, aged look, but at the same time are shellacked, so you never have to worry about getting splinters. It buzzes with energy, and the mindless background chatter makes it a*

terrific place to people-watch and write."

Nathaniel might describe it more like this...

"Brew-n-Bake has one exit and a side door that leads to the kitchen. The tables are spread out with decent lighting, so no one can hide or keep cover in shadows. Taking the seat in the corner would offer a full view of the L-shaped dining area, which would be optimal for watching your back."

Nathaniel and I see the coffee shop as different because we are different people. We notice different things. I don't know anything about fashion, but Nathaniel does. He might pick up on a woman with a coach bag or wearing designer shoes. I, on the other hand, would totally notice someone playing a Nintendo 3DS and might even be able to name the game based on the sound effects or soundtrack.

If you have a point of view problem with your story, start by addressing the prose. Make sure you are telling the novel from the right character's point of view and not your own. It's one of those things that is easier said than done, but as you write more, it's easier to get into the headspace of your characters so that you can see the world as they would.

Assignment: Double check your POV to make sure it doesn't need to be dialed back or fleshed out.

CHECK YOUR TONE

Tone is another huge part of a story. I talked about it briefly when writing about the pitch, but it's worth mentioning again.

If you are doing a grim and dark drama, a poop joke probably doesn't work. Not that you can't have humor, but that kind of humor most likely would break the tone.

Ameriguns was a pain in the butt because it dealt with such serious things. There are several gruesome scenes in the novel, and the protagonist ends up emotionally scarred by them.

At the same time, humor is one of my coping mechanisms and always has been. As bad as I wanted *Ameriguns* to be tough and serious, I couldn't maintain that tone. I ended up with scenes and bits of dialog that were more humorous.

The odd mash-up of dark and humor was broken. Not that they can't work together, but the way handled it in the first draft was too abrupt. There was no ebb and flow to the overall tone.

To fix it, I had to go back and add transitions. Instead of the tone being at a tragic low point and then a paragraph later spike to something silly, I spread it out like a sine wave curve with dropping lines easing between the high points and low points.

If something dark happened, I slowed down the scene before jumping to a scene with more humor. I also made a lot of the humor more character related. For example, scenes with Jay or his daughter were a bit lighter than those with Nathaniel and Vargas.

Of course, sometimes a dark moment needs humor. There is no science to all of this. When I was checking the tone in *Ameriguns*, I was really making sure that the novel had my voice so that someone who has read one of my middle grade novels could pick up *Ameriguns* and say, "Yeah, this feels like Scott."

Consider this book. I wrote *The 5 Day Novel* in my natural speaking voice. This is how I talk. I say strange things like "weird duck," and even though I'm in my thirties, I still think "poop" is a funny word. It cracks me up knowing that, at some point, Eric Michael Summerer, an amazingly talented voice actor, will have to read aloud "I like poop" or "Tom Vasel cheats at board games."

The only way to ensure that the tone is consistent and works in your books is to be aware of your voice and to embrace it. As you write more novels and get to know yourself better, that will become easier.

Until that day happens, watch for transitions and make sure the tone doesn't jump too harshly from one extreme to another. Or if it does make that jump, be sure that it does so in a way that is authentic to your original voice.

Assignment: Check the flow of your tone throughout the novel.

When Is the Book Done?

The magic of doing a 5 Day Novel is that you can't spend five years working on it. You start it, and five days later it is done. If you fail to complete it, then it's not a 5 Day Novel.

I've had students who have told me they have been working on a book for three or four years. I've met would-be-authors who have said they have been writing a novel for decades. That breaks my brain. I write to get the stories out of my head. I can't imagine what would happen if I held the same story in for such a long time.

I knew *Ameriguns* was done because I didn't have a choice. On DAY FOUR, it got to around 11:50 p.m. Before I had to call it quits. I could have tweaked dialog and those kind of things for hours, but if I stayed up any later, it meant I would be too tired to function on DAY FIVE.

Beyond the call of sleep, I knew I was done because the story was there. I'd removed the plot holes. I made sure the character arcs worked. The tone, the dialog, all of it was in a functional state. If I weren't doing a 5 Day Novel, the book was at the point where I would have sent it to my alpha readers.

But since I have a deadline, and I didn't have time for alpha readers, I called it. I locked the story, turning off that side of my brain and knew that, when I woke up on DAY FIVE, I'd have to polish and deal with line editing.

As a writer, at some point you have to say, "This book is the best it's going to be." Remember, no book is perfect. No author is perfect. Only you can know when you've reached that point, but because of the ticking clock, be sure you don't take too long to get there.

Assignment: Finish fixing and doing all the high concept rewrites for your novel.

DAY FOUR JOURNAL

This is the blog post I wrote in the evening of DAY FOUR while writing my 5 Day Novel...

Today was all about the second rewrite...

I'm from the camp who believes the cliche that writing is rewriting, so it was SUPER important that when scheduling my week that I made time for multiple rewrites. No matter how well you plan or outline, things happen when writing. A character whom you thought would do one thing does something completely different, and rewrites allow you to embrace those kinds of changes.

So my main focus today was to fix all the plot and character problems. I did have a few. The core of my story didn't change from the original outline, but the genre unsuspectingly did. I meant the book to contain way more action, like *Taken* or the Jason Bourne movies. I included action, but it's a slower political thriller burn like *The Pelican Brief* or a Brad Meltzer book.

I had so much to do with the characters, and I'm still not done with them. When you start a first draft, they are all new, and you don't know them yet. Now that I know the story and have been through it a few times, I've started to hear their voices. That means I still need to go back again and make sure that those voices are clear and distinct throughout the whole novel.

Lisa is working late night tonight (plant emergency, but not like she's in-danger emergency), so I should have till midnight or later to keep working. My plan is to keep doing passes, addressing and cleaning up all the character bits. Then tomorrow, I'll do a final line-editing pass, which for me is always the hardest and slowest stage of writing a book.

Four days in, and I am feeling burned out. I'm ready to be done. Why couldn't I call this *The 4 Day novel?* so that I could quit or *The 8 Day Novel*, so I could take a break? Uhhhh tomorrow will be painful, but I'm almost done. ONLY ONE MORE DAY!

DAY FOUR CHECKLIST

- ◆ **Assignment:** Make a list of all the problems in your novel and how you will address them.
- ◆ **Assignment:** Fix the big holes in your plot and make sure the theme and message you are trying to get across comes through loud and clear.
- ◆ **Assignment:** Fix any character problems that you find after evaluating the story.
- ◆ **Assignment:** Make a dialog pass on your novel, cleaning it up and fixing character voices.
- ◆ **Assignment:** Double check your POV to make sure it doesn't need to be dialed back or fleshed out.
- ◆ **Assignment:** Check the flow of your tone throughout the novel.
- ◆ **Assignment:** Finish fixing and doing all the high concept rewrites for your novel.

Day Five: The Polish

DAY FIVE PLANS

DAY FIVE is all about getting the book to its final stage. At this point, the story is set. The characters are fixed. There shouldn't be any plot, structure, or creative problems in your novel. It's time to hang up your writer hat officially and don your editor hat because today we are going to do nothing but line edits!

For those of you who don't know, line editing is when you go through and look at every sentence in your book. You ignore plot, characters, and all those things and only worry about the words.

Line editing is about making sure the descriptions are clear, removing any clunky bits, and perfecting your word choice.

Overused Words

Every writer has certain words or phrases they repeat in their work. When writing fiction, I over use the word "just" and say "instead" too often. For example...

> *Nathaniel squared his stance, readying to block the punch, but it didn't come. Instead, the crook kneed him in the groin.*

That is a lame paragraph, but it serves as a good example of how I overuse "instead." I fit it in when something happens that the POV character wasn't expecting. As is, using it the way I do once or twice is not a big deal, but if I do it multiple times per page, it will feel repetitive.

Another word I overuse is "that." I don't know why, but I

regularly substitute it for other pronouns. There is nothing ungrammatical about doing it, but it lowers the clarity of my writing.

At the end of the day, does cutting out overused words make a huge difference? No, but it makes enough of a difference. If a reader notices how you frequently use "that," every time they see it, it may raise a red flag and distract them from the plot and characters. You don't want that. That would be bad 'cause that isn't what you want. See what I did there? I used "that" way too many times in this paragraph.

Finding all your overused words can be simple. Most writing software will give you word distribution stats so you can easily see how many times you use a word.

When I checked the stats for my 110k word fantasy novel, I discovered I'd used "that" 1,400 times. Way too many. I had already done my major line edits, so the only way I could trim the "thats" was by using control+F on my Mac to search for them. It took me a full day, but I managed to cut the "thats" in half!

To me, spending a full day clearing those out was well worth it. You might not feel the same way. That's alright. There is no right or wrong with writing, and there is even less right and wrong with line editing. You will have to judge for yourself how important it is to pull out overused words.

Here is the list of words I searched for while editing *Ameriguns*. I made a mental note, and when I came across them while line editing, I determined if they could be cut or if the sentence should be rewritten. Keep in mind that this list is very specific to me and my faults. Because authors, like characters, have different voices, your list of overused words might overlap with mine, but it should also be different.

That, Even, Equally, Jump, Charge, Run, Walk, Leapt, Shamble, Turn, Look, Glanced, Reach, Instead, Down, Was, Were, Is, Am, Had, Have, A Lot, Then, Thing, Big, Small, Got, Almost, Nearly, Really, About, Actually, Began, Started, Better, Saw, Thought, Also

Just because you overuse a word doesn't mean you shouldn't use it. We will talk about passive voice in a hot second, but I've had students who, once they learned about the passive voice, tried to remove every instance of it from their work. It made their writing feel stilted and unreadable. So if you are going to eliminate overused words, do it with a scalpel and not a sledge hammer.

Assignment: Figure out which words you overuse so that you can remove any unnecessary ones while you line edit.

WEAK VERBS

The difference between a weak verb and a strong verb is how much they can bench press. A strong verb can lift a whole sentence, elevating it to another level, while a weak verb leaves a sentence feeling blah.

Verbs are the key to writing. Using the right one in the right place shows the difference between a novice writer and an advanced one.

Nathaniel walked across the street.

"Walked" is the verb in the previous sentence, and it's a fairly weak one. Even if we doctor up the rest of the sentence, it will still read weak.

Nathaniel walked across the cobbled street, his steel-toed boots clicking against the stone.

Even though we made the sentence fancier, "walk" still comes off weak because it's not specific. If you picture someone walking in your head and I picture someone walking in my head, we both could end up picturing totally different things.

The way to make a weak verb stronger is to get more specific. How is Nathaniel walking across the street? Is it more of a sprint, is he taking longer strides, is he barreling through a dense crowd, does he have a bounce in his step because he's happy?

Being specific with your verbs paints a clearer picture. A character can hold a kitten, and they can hold a gun. If I wanted to be more specific, I could say that a character cradled a kitten. Technically, someone could also cradle a gun, but unless they are creepy, and that is what you are going for, it really doesn't work.

Although "walk" may be weak, there are times when you might want to use it. Remember this:

Nathaniel walked across the cobbled street, his steel-toed boots clicking against the stone.

If the point of the sentence is not the action, I might want to leave walk. Walk is a bland word, and if I want to focus on the cobbled streets and appeal to sound, then I might want to leave walk so as not to distract the reader from the rest of the sentence. When looking to swap weak verbs for stronger ones, focus on verbs that get your point across, but as with overused words, be careful.

Assignment: Figure out the weak verbs you overuse.

Passive Voice

Passive voice gets a bad wrap. A lot of new writers don't know what it is, and once they learn, they think it's evil and that it must be removed or your novel will be bad.

To make sure we are all on the same page, let's look real quick at what passive voice is. Here is an example…

Nathaniel was shot by a barber.

Passive voice is when a sentence is structured so that the thing being acted upon comes before the thing that is performing the action. In the example, the barber is the one doing the action, so to fix the passive voice, we would need to put him at the start of the sentence.

The barber shot Nathaniel.

Removing the to-be verb "was" makes the sentence stronger and flow better. Like overused words, or weak verbs, using the passive voice too often can become a distraction for readers.

It seems super easy to remove passive voice, but sometimes it gets complicated. If the example had been...

Nathaniel was shot.

Removing the passive voice here isn't so easy. You can't simply flip the sentence. You have to rewrite it to be something like...

The bullet tore through Nathaniel's calf.

The second sentence is stronger and action oriented. It's more specific and creates a picture for the reader to see. However, there are times when you might want to use passive voice. Passive voice works well when you want to be mysterious or hold something back so that the reader doesn't discover something until the end of the sentence.

Based on your voice as an author, you'll have to decide how often you want to use passive voice. Whatever you do though, don't cut it all out, but make sure that when you use it, you are using it for a reason.

Assignment: Decide how you will handle passive voice when doing your line edits.

COLORS & BIG WORDS

I'm a sucker for the names of colors because I have a weird thing where I overuse generic colors. I will use red a hundred times in a book, and one of the things I like to do when line editing is to swap out generic colors for more specific ones.

If there I describe a building as red, and I truly mean red, I might leave it, but chances are, the building was actually terracotta or rust colored. Or maybe the blue jacket wasn't actually blue, but was really cobalt or azure.

The problem with tweaking colors in your novel is that it's easy to go too far. If in *Ameriguns* I had written...

Nathaniel wore a flaxen-colored windbreaker.

A lot of people wouldn't know what color flaxen was. If a reader doesn't know, instead of the color helping them to see an image clearly in their mind's eye, it would confuse them. I might be safer using generic yellow or something more relatable like mustard.

The same principle applies to using large words. Novice writers love large words because they want to prove how smart they are. It used to drive me nuts the first year I taught a writing class to be reading a student's work and have to stop and look up a definition of a word. I'm a smart guy. I have an excellent vocabulary, but if big words are slowing me down, then they will really slow down the average reader.

Having to nip those big words in the bud, I prepared a lecture for my class, and I discovered while researching that the reading level for many famous books fluctuates between 6th and 8th grade. These books weren't written at that level because the authors were dumb, but because that's the average reading level for most readers.

I understand the desire to use fancy words, but unless you write literary fiction, you want the prose to be invisible. You readers should focus on the story and characters not on how you used a ten letter word that they didn't know. Adding big words that readers won't understand will confuse them and pull them out of the story.

A reader doesn't care if you can use "perfidious" in a

sentence. They don't need you to prove you are smart. They need you to tell a good story, so instead of using big words, do what we did for colors and weak verbs: use specific words.

Assignment: Check your use of colors and overall vocabulary to make sure they are on par with where you want them and don't distract from the story.

EXCEPTIONS

Writing teachers drill into people that they shouldn't use adverbs. They say things like, "Instead of saying 'she quickly ran,' say, 'she sprinted.'" For the most part, that's true. It always helps to be more specific and to use strong verbs, but at the same time there needs to be a balance.

Using a word like "walk" or "quickly" can serve as a shortcut. Instead of getting bogged down on something that doesn't matter or really can't impact the story, you can move forward and focus your time tweaking the writing that does matter.

When doing a 5 Day Novel, the clock is ticking. You have only so much time to get it done. Also, there is a lot less that you can do as an author in a 45k-word novel than in a 100k-word novel. You might need to take shortcuts when writing, and if you do, that's alright. You are allowed.

Everyone knows that you are supposed to show and not tell, but sometimes telling is so much faster! By telling I can get a point across in half a sentence. There might be times when you choose to tell for the sake of speed and page space.

In *Ameriguns*, I have a scene set at the Cathedral of St. Mathews the Apostle in Washington, D.C. I describe the church this way…

> *On the outside, the Cathedral of St. Mathews the Apostle resembled the famous castle on the National Mall. It had red sandstone walls with a terra-cotta trim while a bronze dome capped a single octagonal tower over its nave.*

It's not very flowy, but it gets the job done. A reader gets the gist of what the cathedral looks like. If I wanted to spend the time to rewrite it, I could turn it into something like this…

> *The Cathedral of St. Mathews the Apostle resembled the famous castle on the National Mall. Red sandstone walls glistened in the dull setting sunlight. The terra-cotta trim contrasted against the dark sandstone blocks, and a single octagonal tower crested above the nave, like a crown perched on a king's head. A bronze dome, dull and weathered capped the Cathedral's tower.*

In the rewrite, I took out the to-be verbs, and I did a lot more showing instead of telling. The trade-off is that the paragraph is almost twice as long, and it took time to rewrite it.

Guess what? In the novel, I choose not to rewrite the paragraph. The reason is I wanted the outside of the Cathedral to come off a bit more bland and dull. The inside of St. Mathews is gorgeous, and I wanted to juxtapose a bland description of the outside with something a bit more flowery for the inside.

All of this goes back to knowing your voice. When doing your line edits, keep in mind that sometimes it's perfectly acceptable to use shortcuts and make exceptions to overused words, weak verbs, or passive voice.

Assignment: Understand that there are exceptions to grammar and style rules, and you should line edit in a way that fits your voice as an author.

LINE EDITING

Certain authors are masters of writing prose. Neil Gaiman can do more in a single sentence than I can in a paragraph. J. K. Rowling and Patrick Rothfuss are two other examples of authors who can write descriptions that at times feel lyrical.

I know I will never be at their level. I will never be able to make words flow off the tongue in the magical way that they can. What I can do is make sure that my prose is clear and not distracting. In the best-case scenario, my descriptions are invisible, and the readers don't even notice them because they are experiencing the story. That's my goal with line editing.

Depending on your goals as an author and your skill level, you may also be shooting for invisible prose, or you may be trying to craft something more special. That's up to you to decide.

Personally, I hate line editing. I loathe it. I used to think it was because I'm dyslexic and, thus struggle with it, but after meeting so many indie authors this past year, I've learned that the majority of writers don't like to do it.

Because the act of line editing is so disliked, it's easy to skip it and send a manuscript to an editor without putting in the work. I think that's a mistake. As much as I despise line editing, I structured the 5 Day Novel so that I could spend all of DAY FIVE doing it.

Getting your manuscript as clean as possible before sending it to an editor means that, instead of worrying about awkward sentences, your editor can focus their attention on other things. You'll end up with a better written novel.

By line editing yourself before passing it on, you also ensure that your voice is clear. Remember when we were cleaning up dialog, and we removed the fluffy bits so that the characters sounded more distinct? The same principle works with line editing. You are removing distracting elements to make your voice clearer.

Assignment: Line edit your novel!

DAY FIVE JOURNAL

This is the blog post I wrote on the evening of DAY FIVE while writing my 5 Day Novel...

Today was all about line editing...

TODAY was rough. I made it through one pass. Then I did a quick word search for some of my crutch words.

I've mentioned before that I underwrite. Part of that is my background is screenwriting. A screenplay is much more sparse than a novel when it comes to descriptions. A screenplay is a blueprint for a final product (the movie), while a book is a final product. So it makes sense that in a novel I need to include many more details.

That meant I spent most of the day rereading every sentence and rewriting as well as fleshing out the details. So "Nathaniel entered the arena. Across the stage he saw the target." would instead become a full paragraph (which I'm too tired to actually write right now). The paragraph would have to flow, have the right depth of POV, and give a general sense of the setting without being too much.

Line editing is what I hate most about writing. If it weren't so important for my own voice and finalizing the story, I'd try to hire someone else to do it. But it matters, and I could, of course, go back and do another full pass now, but at this point, I'm calling it. The book is done.

I exported an epub and sent the file to my two alpha readers. They both promised to have the whole thing read by the 5th. The book is due to my editor on the 8th. As I've said several times this week, the themes and plot deal with some sensitive hot topics. So in this case, the alpha reads are important to make sure I handled those things in a tasteful manner that serves the characters and story I'm trying to tell. I don't expect to have to make any major changes, but I might need to cut a few lines here or there or add a few to clarify descriptions that I thought were clear but ended up being too vague.

But yeah. It's done. I didn't know if I could get the book done. My brain is fried. My body is fried. I feel like I just walked a marathon. This was a fascinating exercise, and I never want to do it again! Glad I did it. Glad that I discovered I could do it, but still NEVER AGAIN.

Now it's time for some well earned sleep.

DAY FIVE CHECKLIST

- **Assignment:** Figure out which words you overuse so that you can remove any unnecessary ones while you line edit.
- **Assignment:** Figure out the weak verbs you overuse.
- **Assignment:** Decide how you will handle passive voice when doing your line edits.
- **Assignment:** Check your use of colors and overall vocabulary to make sure they are on par with where you want them and don't distract from the story.
- **Assignment:** Understand that there are exceptions to grammar and style rules, and you should line edit in a way that fits your voice as an author.
- **Assignment:** Line edit your novel!

Afterword

DONE!

I turned in my 5 Day Novel at 10:33 p.m. on a Friday night. I know I still had ninety minutes left, but I was done. My brain was fried. I was emotionally and physically spent.

I showered, took the puppies out, and then went to bed. Lisa, who had been pinning on Pinterest with her iPad was surprised to see me. She thought for sure I was going to work till midnight or maybe even cheat and continue working till exactly 120 hours from when I had started.

I told her that I was done. I climbed into bed. We cuddled, and I slept soooooo well. On Saturday, I got up early, made Lisa breakfast as a thank you for being so awesome and supportive, and we went to the beach.

It felt so nice to be outside and away from the computer.

Sure I did my five-mile walks every day during the week, but having the novel turned in meant I was no longer in that headspace. I could enjoy the waves and swimming without stressing. A weight was off my shoulders, and I got to enjoy life again.

Coming out of the challenge, it felt like I had time traveled to the future. I hadn't been on social media. I hadn't gone to Brew-n-Bake. I hadn't talked to friends or family on the phone. I hadn't played board games! I felt out of loop with the world.

I didn't know at the start of the challenge how much of a mind game it would be. I thought for sure I would have to push my physical limits. I was pretty certain I would have to block out the pain of blisters or a sore back. But honestly, because I had taken care of myself, my body was fine. It was my brain that felt scrambled.

I almost didn't get the 5 Day Novel done, and at midweek I thought achieving it would be impossible. Looking back, there are things I would change if I could. I would have started writing the first draft on DAY ONE.

Prewriting took me only ten to twelve hours to plan and map out the story. That meant I had another six or so hours I could have used to start getting words on the page.

If I had a redo, I wouldn't have shot for doing 50k words in one day. I know now that I'm not a badass romance author. I'll never be that tough, but that's alright. I'm happy with who I am and what I can do. I just wish I had known up front so I could have used that extra time on DAY ONE.

On DAY TWO, when I failed to get that first draft done in one day, it really crushed me. I was sure at that point that I wouldn't finish the novel. If not for the support of others cheering me on, I would have quit. So allowing for a bit more leniency to decrease the chance of failure would have been nice.

The most shocking thing I discovered while doing the challenge was that it is doable. I took a book from concept, did multiple rewrites, and polished it within five days. Would I do it again? Heck no, but it's sure dang nice knowing that I could if I wanted.

In an ideal world where time didn't matter, I think writing *Ameriguns* over the course of twelve to fifteen weekdays would have been perfect. Doing so would mean that I could enjoy my nights with Lisa and that on the weekends we could have our adventures, which are super important for helping me recharge and feel creative.

What I gained most from doing the 5 Day Novel is a sense of confidence. I know my limits as a writer. I cannot type more than 30k words in a single day, but I learned I'm capable of doing more than the 5k–7k words that I usually do.

This book was supposed to be about 20k words long. My plan was to write it the week after doing the 5 Day Novel. On Wednesday of this week, when I realized I was being a bum and hadn't finished the first draft, I buckled down and got to work. By the end of the day, I hit 31k! The best part is that I didn't have to push that hard and still took the evening off to eat dinner and watch old *Gilmore Girls* episodes with Lisa.

If I hadn't done a novel in five days, it probably would have taken me a full five to seven days to get the first draft of this book done, but because I knew what I was capable of and that I could easily handle it, I was able to get it done at a faster pace.

I have no regrets about attempting the challenge. Doing so allowed me to streamline my workflow and learn my limits. I'm glad I did it.

Publishing Ameriguns

I knew at a very young age who I was and came to terms with it very quickly. I loved the beach and swimming, but hated sand because it is basically dirt. That awareness of who I am has led me to be confident in my day-to day-life, but damn I still get nervous every time I publish a book.

If you want to read *Ameriguns*, the novel I wrote in five days, you can. It's right here on Amazon.

Because I'm writing this nonfiction book before my editor has given *Ameriguns* back to me, I'm not sure what has changed since I turned it in, but I know there was nothing major.

Of my two alpha readers, one had a family emergency and didn't have time to read the novel before I turned it into my editor. The other was useful. I used their reactions to judge how some of the sensitive topics in the novel were handled. I dialed the details for one back, but left the rest as was.

That's really what I'm most nervous about. I designed *Ameriguns* around the theme of gun violence. In the book there is murder, horrific events, tragedy, and an underlying commentary about the media. There is no way to know how people will react to the novel until they read it.

As important as the hot topics are, I did my best to not be preachy. While writing, I always put story and character first, but deep down, I'm nervous. What if someone picks it up and thinks my only goal was to exploit the hot topic gun of violence? That would be horrible 'cause it was never my intent to milk such big social issues. I wrote the novel because I wasn't sure how I felt, and it was a way for me to work through my feelings.

My hope is that people pick up *Ameriguns* and fly through it, wanting to know what happens to Nathaniel or to see the next stupid thing that Jay says. If at the same time it makes them ponder the themes I touch upon, that's great, but first and foremost, I hope people enjoy it.

No matter how it is perceived, I'm proud of *Ameriguns*. It hurts to watch the news. It hurts to talk to law enforcement and hear the horrors they've seen this past summer. I wrote the novel from my heart. It became a story that I felt passionate about telling. My fingers are crossed that the readers get that.

Hitting the button to publish a book is scary, but if I didn't want people to read it, then there was no point in writing it. I don't know if *Ameriguns* will stand the test of time. Five years from now I may think it's poop, but that's what it's like being an author. All you can do is judge where you are now and work hard at making sure it's the best it can be.

It's funny how books change as you write them. On the Monday when I was dreaming up the world and characters, I had a vision for what *Ameriguns* would feel like, but as stories do, it grew and became its own thing. Now it's done, and I'm going to set it loose upon the world as an ebook, print book, and audiobook. I feel like a parent dropping a kid off on the first day of school. It's a nerve-racking, but great feeling, and one I hope you get to experience.

I have said it numerous times. Writing isn't easy. It takes stubbornness and a passion to commit to it, but you know what? I have faith in you. If you truly want to be a writer, you don't need to write a novel in five days, but you do need to write.

Please go out there and make the world a better place by sharing your unique view of it. No one else can tell the stories that you want to tell, and it would be a shame if you never told them.

NOTE TO THE READER

Thank you for reading *The 5 Day Novel*. If you enjoyed the book, I hope you'll consider **leaving a review**. They're the lifeblood of indie authors and the most important factor other readers use to decide if they will pick it up.

ABOUT THE AUTHOR

Scott King is a writer, photographer, and educator. He was born in Washington D.C., and raised in Ocean City, Maryland. He received his undergraduate degree in film from Towson University and his M.F.A. in film from American University.

"DAD! A Documentary Graphic Novel," Scott's first book, was published in Fall '09. He is the creator and writer of "Holiday Wars," and he is known for his board game photography, specifically his annual calendar that highlights card and hobby games.

To learn more about Scott and his work, visit his website at www.ScottKing.info. You can also follow him on twitter via @ScottKing.

44883512R00111

Made in the USA
San Bernardino, CA
23 July 2019